FICTION AND RESEARCH

Creative Research Methods in Practice

Series Editor: **Helen Kara**, We Research It Ltd.

This dynamic series presents short practical books by and for researchers around the world on how to use creative and innovative research methods from apps to zines. Edited by the leading independent researcher Helen Kara, it is the first series to provide guidance on using creative research methods across all disciplines.

Scan the code below to discover new and forthcoming titles in the series, or visit:

bristoluniversitypress.co.uk/
creative-research-methods-in-practice

FICTION AND RESEARCH

A Guide to Connecting Stories and Inquiry

Becky Tipper and Leah Gilman

First published in Great Britain in 2024 by

Policy Press, an imprint of
Bristol University Press
University of Bristol
1–9 Old Park Hill
Bristol
BS2 8BB
UK
t: +44 (0)117 374 6645
e: bup-info@bristol.ac.uk

Details of international sales and distribution partners are available at
policy.bristoluniversitypress.co.uk

© Bristol University Press 2024

British Library Cataloguing in Publication Data
A catalogue record for this book is available from the British Library

ISBN 978-1-4473-6972-1 hardcover
ISBN 978-1-4473-6973-8 paperback
ISBN 978-1-4473-6974-5 ePub
ISBN 978-1-4473-6975-2 ePdf

The right of Becky Tipper and Leah Gilman to be identified as authors of this work has been asserted by them in accordance with the Copyright, Designs and Patents Act 1988.

All rights reserved: no part of this publication may be reproduced, stored in a retrieval system, or transmitted in any form or by any means, electronic, mechanical, photocopying, recording, or otherwise without the prior permission of Bristol University Press.

Every reasonable effort has been made to obtain permission to reproduce copyrighted material. If, however, anyone knows of an oversight, please contact the publisher.

The statements and opinions contained within this publication are solely those of the authors and not of the University of Bristol or Bristol University Press. The University of Bristol and Bristol University Press disclaim responsibility for any injury to persons or property resulting from any material published in this publication.

Bristol University Press and Policy Press work to counter discrimination on grounds of gender, race, disability, age and sexuality.

Cover design: Qube Design
Front cover image: iStock/Veronika Oliinyk

Contents

List of figures vi
Acknowledgements vii

PART I Thinking about fiction and research
1 Tracing connections between fiction and research 3
2 Theoretical approaches to fiction and research 23

PART II Fiction in practice
3 Examples of fiction in practice 43
4 Difficult questions 77

PART III Creating and sharing fiction
5 Crafting fictions: practical notes and creative prompts 99
6 Next steps: sharing research-fictions 125

Notes 135
References 137
Index 153

List of figures

1.1	Anthropologist and writer Zora Neale Hurston	5
1.2	Philosopher and novelist Iris Murdoch	7
1.3	Physicist and writer Alan Lightman	8
3.1	'In the rain': scene from 'Train Alone Day'	52
3.2	Actors Alison Belbin and Paul Nolan playing Joyce and Jim in a production of *Passing On*, along with the puppet which represented Joyce's mother	57
3.3	Layla's family grapples with the possibility of kidney donation	61
3.4	News of Anna's mother's diagnosis spreads at Anna's school	63

Acknowledgements

Many people have offered inspiration and support, in various forms and at various times, as we developed this book and the ideas that inform it. We are especially grateful to Abbie Killeen, Helen Kara, Katherine Ellsworth-Krebs, Paul Stevens, Verónica Policarpo, the anonymous peer reviewers of our proposal and manuscript, speakers and participants who attended the Writing Sociological Fiction workshop at the University of Manchester, and all members of the Morgan Centre, particularly Petra Nordqvist and Jennifer Mason. And to our respective partners and children, Jeremy, Clem and Ushi, and Alex, Niamh and Sam, thank you for your love, encouragement and practical support – without which this book would not have been written.

We also gratefully acknowledge funding from the Morgan Centre for Research into Everyday Life and the University of Manchester School of Social Sciences for earlier workshops, collaborations and activities from which the ideas in this book have developed.

PART I

Thinking about fiction and research

1

Tracing connections between fiction and research

This chapter:

- Traces the parallels between the aims and practice of researchers and fiction writers.
- Presents case studies of writers who have combined fiction and research.
- Introduces our definition of fiction.
- Suggests further reading on storytelling and fiction.
- Outlines the book's structure.

Introduction

This book is an invitation to researchers of all kinds to explore the possibilities of fiction.

At first glance, fiction and research might seem diametrically opposed. Whereas research (in its many forms) aims to generate an understanding of the real world, fiction is, by definition, 'made up'. Research deals with facts, and fiction with inventions. How, then, can they speak to one another? How can fiction inform research? And what would it mean to bring fiction into the practice or dissemination of research? These are the questions that guide this book (and we think they have some compelling answers for researchers across a wide range of disciplines and backgrounds).

We use the term 'research' broadly, to refer to the systematic study of a question or topic which aims to understand or address that topic or question. Throughout the chapters that follow, we will discuss innovative, intriguing and diverse ways that researchers in diverse disciplines might engage – and have engaged – with fiction.

We do not think that there is one 'right way' to connect research and fiction – our intention is not to argue for any particular role that fiction should play (such as writing a novel about one's own data). Instead, in this book, we aim to showcase a range of possibilities, encourage researchers to think creatively and critically about the potentials of fiction, and point researchers in the direction of some of the resources they might need to start out on the journey of incorporating stories into their work.

In this chapter, we take some first steps by tracing a variety of connections between fiction and research – opening up ways to think about these two forms, asking what fiction might offer to researchers, and highlighting points of contact which already exist between them. We also look more closely at what we (and others) mean by 'fiction' and outline some defining characteristics and components of fictional stories, which will inform our discussions throughout this book.

From research to fiction: writers who have forged a path

When thinking about connections between research and fiction, one useful starting point is to consider the work of researchers who *also* created well-known fiction, in many cases drawing on knowledge gained from their research.

There are many striking examples. Astrophysicist Carl Sagan authored the 1985 novel *Contact* (the basis of Robert Zemeckis' 1997 film), a story which imagines humanity's first contact with intelligent extra-terrestrial life. It was Jenna Blum's work as a researcher for the Shoah Foundation, collecting Holocaust survivors' oral narratives, that led her to write two best-selling novels inspired by those histories: *Those Who Save Us* (2004) and *The Lost Family* (2018). Ann Oakley – a British sociologist known for her academic research on feminism, housework and motherhood – has authored several novels, including *The Men's Room* (1988), which was adapted into a BBC television series. John Berger's theory and criticism profoundly influenced humanities and social science research (particularly art history and animal studies), but he also wrote numerous novels and genre-defying works, including the Booker Prize-winning *G.* (1972). During the 20th century, physical chemist and novelist C.P. Snow's career spanned both scientific research and literature, although he famously lamented that the 'two cultures' – science and the literary arts – were too polarised and that practitioners in each form rarely crossed the divide (Snow 2012). And, in the 1920s and 1930s, Zora Neale Hurston studied anthropology as a postgraduate (under the supervision of Franz Boas and alongside Margaret Mead), although she is widely remembered for her fiction, including the novel *Their Eyes Were Watching God* (1937) (Figure 1.1). In fact, much of Hurston's research *itself* concerned fiction and storytelling, in the form of oral tales and folklore among Black people in the southern US and the Caribbean.

Figure 1.1: Anthropologist and writer Zora Neale Hurston

Source: 'Portrait of Zora Neale Hurston – Eatonville, Florida. 1900 (circa)', State Archives of Florida, Florida Memory, https://www.floridamemory.com/items/show/33048

However, while Hurston's fiction seems to have been informed by her academic work and research, it is interesting to note that she later reflected that her aim in writing fiction was to convey the richness and humanity of Black lives, and not to produce 'a treatise on sociology' (Gates 2013 [1937]: 200).[1]

Hurston's reflections hint at some of the connections (and tensions) that researchers might encounter when they create fiction. Not all researchers who have crossed the research/fiction divide (including many of those listed previously) have publicly articulated how and why they chose to do so. However, Iris Murdoch, who achieved renown as both a philosopher and novelist (Box 1.1) and Alan Lightman, a contemporary physicist and writer (Box 1.2), have both reflected insightfully on the relationship (and differences) between scholarly research and fiction. And, as we now discuss, their reflections offer some useful pointers for tracing connections between these two forms.

Box 1.1: Iris Murdoch on literature and academic writing

Iris Murdoch (1919–1999) (Figure 1.2) was a moral philosopher and the author of 26 acclaimed novels, including *The Sea, The Sea*, which won the Booker Prize in 1978.

In the essay collection *Existentialists and Mystics* (1999), Murdoch reflects on the nature of literature and scholarly writing, and how each medium communicates and examines ideas. She argues that whereas academic writers seek to explain, codify and shed light on a topic, fiction often works to 'mystify' a reader (Murdoch 1999: 5).

As Murdoch observes, 'the literary writer leaves a space for his reader to play in' (1999: 5). In contrast to the closure of academic texts, a successful piece of fiction embraces open-endedness and possibility: 'a great work of art gives one a sense of space, as if one had been invited into some large hall of reflection' (1999: 28). For Murdoch, literature and other works of art often evoke fear and awe, which are key to their potency: 'art is close dangerous play with unconscious forces. We enjoy art, even simple art, because it disturbs us in deep often incomprehensible ways' (1999: 10).

Figure 1.2: Philosopher and novelist Iris Murdoch

Source: Everett Collection Historical/Alamy Stock Photo

However, while literary fiction stands in contrast to scholarly writing, the two modes also share certain qualities. Murdoch reflects that they are 'both truth-seeking and truth-revealing activities. They are cognitive activities, explanations. ... Art is cognition in another mode. Think how much thought, how much truth, a Shakespeare play contains, or a great novel' (1999: 11).

Literature, for Murdoch – with its connections to the 'unconscious' and 'mystifying' – has an almost otherworldly quality (something reflected in her own novels). However, she also observes that it occupies a central space in everyday life:

> Literary modes are very natural to us, very close to ordinary life and to the way we live as reflective beings. [They involve] ... invention, masks, playing roles, pretending, imagining, story-telling. When we return home and 'tell our day', we are artfully shaping material into story form. (These stories are very often funny, incidentally.) (1999: 6)

Fiction, then, is one way in which – like research, and like ordinary storytelling – we might make sense of the world around us.

Box 1.2: Alan Lightman on science and fiction

Alan Lightman (Figure 1.3), who currently teaches at Massachusetts Institute of Technology, is a physicist and author of popular science books and novels. His first novel, *Einstein's Dreams* (1993) – which combines biographical fiction, scientific theory and fantastical speculation – steps inside Albert Einstein's mind during the time Einstein was working on the general theory of relativity. The novel consists of a series of shorter scenes, each of which imagines a different way in which time could function.

Figure 1.3: Physicist and writer Alan Lightman

Source: 'Alan by Michael Lionstar' by Lightmanalan1 is licensed under CC BY-SA 4.0, https://creativecommons.org/licenses/by-sa/4.0/

Analysing the differences between fiction and non-fiction, Lightman emphasises fiction's capacity to engage and affect. He observes that 'If you want a person to really care about something, intellectual or not, you need to hit him or her in the amygdala. Reading a novel is a far different experience from reading a book on history or astrophysics' (Newberger Goldstein and Lightman 2011: 34).

This difference is characterised, he notes, by a profound feeling of immersion in a fictional world and its characters:

> [W]hen we read a novel, we are taken to the scene, we smell the scent of linseed oil, we hear the cracking voice of a grandfather,

> we see the smoke rising from a burning house in the distance. We feel the joy and suffering of good characters. Either consciously or unconsciously, we enter the world created by the novelist and experience things at a visceral level. Words and actions and scenes make an emotional impression on us and that impression is deep. (2011: 34)

However, although fiction offers something that most academic writing does not, Lightman also suggests that there are parallels between scientific inquiry and fiction-writing. Evocatively, he proposes that novels can be viewed as 'emotional experiments', and he suggests that:

> You, the writer, should, after putting your characters in a difficult situation, stand back and wait and listen, and eventually your characters will react in an authentic and sometimes surprising way. It is always good when a character surprises the writer, because then you know you have done an honest experiment and found out something new. (2011: 35)

For Lightman, then, fiction is at once a means to *examine* the world and a way to *reach* readers on an emotional level.

The potentials of fiction

Lightman's and Murdoch's reflections on the power of fiction, and their observations about commonalities between practices of research and storytelling, underscore a key idea which we will explore throughout this book – namely, that fiction has the potential to enable researchers to achieve many of the things they may aim to achieve through their research.

Such potential might be realised in various ways. For instance, Iris Murdoch's comment about 'how much truth' is contained in literature captures a common sentiment about fiction. Author Neil Gaiman (echoing Albert Camus) similarly observes that 'fiction is the lie that tells the truth' (Gaiman 2016: 13). Such 'truth/s' might concern how the social world works, how people do (or should) act, or the phenomenal experience of what life *feels like*. Truths about real life might be found even in stories which are not remotely realistic – Bruno Bettelheim argues that the fantastical worlds of fairy tales convey powerful psychological truths about human relationships, where 'the child intuitively comprehends that although these stories are *unreal*, they are not *untrue*' (1989: 73, emphasis in original). To the extent that researchers also wish to access and illuminate 'truths' about the social or interpersonal world, fiction might offer one way to do this. And, indeed, as Lightman and Murdoch suggest, it may be much *more* effective than non-fictional writing at capturing open-ended, emotional or subtle 'truths'.

Illuminating the world through research also entails putting it into words. A common aim of researchers is to generate language which might allow them to recognise, categorise and discuss phenomena or processes. Some such terms, of course, have entered into the popular lexicon – 'cultural capital' and 'cognitive dissonance' are two examples. However, fiction *also* provides a powerful way to articulate or identify ideas and experiences. Fictional films and novels are the origin of terms such as 'gaslighting', 'a glitch in the matrix', 'doublethink', 'newspeak' and 'catch-22' – complex concepts which, when named and concretised within the context of a fictional story, can be discussed and widely understood, and may have the potential to reach and impact many more people than an academic or traditional research output.

Fiction might also have potential to help researchers share their work in particularly impactful ways. Fiction can be arresting and resonant and might transport a reader to a world or set of circumstances, and the reader's emotional involvement with a fictional character can generate a vivid, sympathetic understanding, perhaps more powerfully than other forms of writing. For researchers who, in Lightman's words, hope to 'make people really care about' their work, fiction might offer one way to achieve this aim.

This impact might be realised not only via individual readers' emotions, but also in terms of the wider *reach* of a fictional work. Since researchers also often wish to bring their ideas to a broad audience and stimulate discussion, fiction's ability to capture the public imagination may be very appealing. Recent examples of particularly impactful fiction include Kristen Roupenian's (2017) 'Cat Person' – a candid short story about a New York woman's sexual encounter – which garnered over four million hits and ignited global conversations about consent (Brockes 2019), and Charlie Brooker's Netflix series *Black Mirror*, which has had a resounding influence on debates about the social consequences of technology (McSweeney and Joy 2019). In such cases, fictional works seem to offer a uniquely potent way to communicate issues to a wide audience and generate engaged discourse.

Fiction, then, offers potential ways to articulate truths, communicate concepts, impact readers and engage audiences – issues of key concern to many researchers. And, as we will explore in the chapters that follow, these potentials have been the driving force behind many researchers' efforts to connect their work with fiction or fictional forms.

Fiction and research: points of contact

Another useful way to trace connections between fiction and research is to reflect on their history of cross-pollination – the various ways, across various disciplines, that *points of contact* have been established, or have emerged, between them.

One distinctive point of contact is found in theoretical arguments (in the social sciences and humanities) about the construction of the fact/fiction binary itself. It can be argued that for much of human history, myth, religion and storytelling have played a significant role in making sense of the world, and have not always been distinguished from formal research. However, the advent of the European Enlightenment in the 17th and 18th centuries – with its emphasis on rationality, objectivity, reason, truth and observable facts – marked the beginning of a stark conceptual divide between the empirical 'real world' and imagined, or fictional, worlds (see, for example, Clifford and Marcus 1986; Richardson 1997a; Snow 2012; Toliver 2021). As we explore further in Chapter 2, for many researchers, engaging with fiction is one way to challenge Enlightenment binaries. Arguably, such thinking represents not so much a 'point of contact' as a querying of the idea that fiction and research are distinctive 'points' in the first place.

In social science research, connections with fiction can be seen most clearly in the ongoing practice of anonymisation or the creation of composite characters to protect the identities of participants (Markham 2012). But there are other more markedly literary points of contact between fiction and the social and psychological sciences. For instance, Sigmund Freud heavily fictionalised his psychoanalytic case studies in order to capture their complexities (Cohn 1999; Watson 2011; Rabbiosi and Vanolo 2017: 51). Similarly, some mid-20th century social anthropologists turned to the 'ethnographic novel' – featuring fictionalised characters and a literary style – to convey their findings (Bowen 1964; Schmidt 1984). Additionally, during the 19th and early 20th centuries, the emergent discipline of sociology was closely linked with the rise of realist or 'social problem' novels. These novels exposed the impoverished conditions of urban life in industrialised societies, raising wide awareness of such issues and even informing the theories and approaches taken by social scientists and reformers (for example, Lepenies 1988; Ponzio 2021; and see discussion in Watson 2016). Taken together, such social and psychological examples show how fiction has, in various ways, enabled readers to 'care about', and perhaps more fully understand, some of the human experiences depicted by researchers.

In other disciplines, the imagined worlds of fiction sometimes connect with real-world research. Science fiction, of course, often draws on and explores established scientific knowledge. Occasionally, it may specifically aim to communicate that knowledge – astronomer Johannes Kepler wrote the allegorical tale *The Dream* (sometimes considered to be the first work of science-based fiction) in order to introduce the Copernican model of the universe to a sceptical 17th-century audience (Popova 2019). However, fictional ideas might also influence scientific discourse or even suggest avenues for investigation. For instance, science-fiction author Arthur C. Clarke is widely credited with inventing global communications satellites, having first written about such technology in 1945, and it has been suggested that the holographic interface screens depicted in the 2002 film *Minority Report* inspired subsequent touchscreen design (Bleecker 2009; Bassett et al 2013). In these instances, fiction again seems to play a role not only in communicating research-based ideas, but also, potentially, in shaping research.

Another intriguing point of contact is the history of thought experiments, which philosophers and scientists have used as a method of inquiry from antiquity to the present (for example, Stuart et al 2018). Thought experiments invite us to imagine a host of fictional scenarios. For instance, the body of a famous violinist has been grafted onto your own without your knowledge or consent, and the violinist is now dependent on you to stay alive (Thomson's violinist, a thought experiment on the ethics of abortion). A supernatural being is able to control the movement of gas molecules between two chambers (Maxwell's demon, on the second law of thermodynamics). A cat – sealed in a chamber along with a decaying radioactive substance – might be both alive and dead at once (Schrodinger's cat, on the concept of superpositions in quantum theory). These fictions – invented scenarios which have never happened and perhaps never could happen – show how stories can be used to interrogate research-based claims and develop hypotheses to guide future research. Moreover, for some theorists, thought experiments do not only illuminate pre-existing facts, but actually generate new knowledge, and as such might even be seen as a *form of research* in themselves (Falk 2017).

In Chapter 2, we explore in more depth a range of disciplinary and theoretical arguments for the use of fiction. However, as these examples suggest, the role of fiction in research is not necessarily new or untested. In some cases, fictional approaches can be seen as already entwined (perhaps surprisingly) in the history and practice of some research areas, and fiction may have already played a role in informing, shaping, producing or communicating research ideas.

Defining fiction

In our discussion so far, although we have used the word 'fiction' frequently, we have not yet defined what we, and others, mean by it, but it is useful at this point to reflect on some of the word's complexities and connotations. While 'fiction' often refers to printed or performed stories about imagined events and characters (as we discuss later), it does not *only* refer to literary outputs.

In ordinary speech, 'fiction' can also refer more generally to inventions or constructs. Consider, for instance, the maintenance of 'a polite fiction' (tacitly overlooking an uncomfortable truth); 'a fiction' as an exaggeration or illusion; or the concept of a 'legal fiction' (for example, that corporations are persons). Such meanings underline the ways in which the concept of 'fiction' extends far beyond novels, plays or films.

Similarly, the 'points of contact' we have discussed highlight subtly different meanings and applications of 'fiction' in research, and we suggest the following three broad, and frequently overlapping, categories are useful for thinking about these uses:

1. Researchers may add invented details or change aspects of otherwise empirical data (as seen in anonymised social science accounts and Freud's case studies) – a practice of *fictionalisation*.
2. In some cases, research is informed or communicated by fully realised *works of fiction*, such as novels, and the ideas contained within them (for example, where science-fiction stories inform research, or where social realist novels overlap with sociological theories and concerns).
3. Sometimes research involves asking 'what if?" questions, which invite people to speculate and imagine things which are not true (as in thought experiments), an engagement with fiction that we call *fictional thinking*.[2]

Throughout this book, we explore how researchers have engaged with fiction in these varied ways. In some instances, 'fiction' involves just one of these categories, while in other cases, all three meanings might apply.

It follows then that connecting fiction and research does not necessarily mean writing a publishable novel or a staging a play based on research data – many more possibilities exist. Nevertheless, works of fiction *are* of interest to many researchers, and it is important to look more closely at what exactly such works involve, especially if researchers wish to produce them. What do readers and audiences expect from works of fiction? What defines fictional stories, and what elements do they typically contain? In the following section, we outline some important characteristics that many works of fiction share – whether they are told through written, visual or performative media.

Elements of fictional stories

We are mindful that many words have different meanings when used by literary critics, academics, writers and lay-people, so it is useful to clarify some of the terms we will use throughout this book. Following the *Cambridge English Dictionary* (2023), we define 'story' simply as 'a description, either true or imagined, of a connected series of events'. There is a significant overlap with 'narrative', which is similarly defined as 'a story or a description of a series of events'. But, for our purposes, we would also suggest that 'stories' are united by an aim (perhaps alongside other aims) to entertain, enlighten or affect the audience to whom they are told. (Consider, for instance, how the phrase 'tell me a story' conveys a meaning that 'tell me a narrative' does not.) Stories and storytelling (like narratives) might be non-fictional, but we focus here mainly on fictional stories – depicting invented or imagined characters and/or events – which might be told through a variety of media, including written prose, comics, oral tales, plays, films, animations and TV series (and, as we will discuss, there is a rich literature about what exactly makes a 'good' story).[3] Finally, we note that fictional stories are usually 'plotted' – their events structured and conveyed in a meaningful way, linked through chains of consequences and meaning. These plots are told through story structures (or dramatic structures), which often take a number of common forms.

For instance, stories may be told in three dramatic acts – a beginning, middle and end; or rising action, conflict and resolution (Aristotle 1997: 14; McKee 1997; Storr 2020). Stories might also fall into five acts (as in many Shakespearean plays and in tragic drama known as Freytag's pyramid), with an introduction or exposition; a rising movement; a climax; falling action; and finally, a resolution or denouement (an explanation or the tying up of loose ends) or in the case of a tragedy, a final catastrophe (for example, Fox 2020; Storr 2020). Another commonly identified template is that of the 'hero's journey', 'monomyth' or 'quest' story (McKee 1997; Vogler 2007), which can be traced to mythical tales of ancient Greek heroes, although it need not feature a male protagonist. Here, a character in their ordinary world receives a 'call to adventure' and embarks on a quest, meets mentors and allies on the way, is challenged and tested, enters an 'innermost cave' where they engage in battle or endure an ordeal, before eventually returning home with an 'elixir' – perhaps a literal treasure or magical potion, or figuratively, the rewards of experience and wisdom (Vogler 2007). The hero's journey can be seen clearly in works of fiction such as J.R.R. Tolkien's *The Hobbit*.

While these structures appear in stories throughout the world, there are also cultural variations. For instance, while Western stories traditionally revolve around an individual hero battling external forces, Eastern stories often emphasise community and a quest for harmony, and the *kishōtenketsu* structure of Japanese, Korean and Chinese fiction breaks narratives into not five, but four acts: an introduction, a development, a surprising and unexpected twist, and an ambiguous final act where the audience is left to make sense of the story (Storr 2020: 83; Salesses 2021: 107).

These structures can be useful to 'think with' and may help writers to craft stories. However, they should not be seen as prescriptive, nor as independent of other aspects of fiction, such as characters and their development. As Will Storr notes, the five-act structure is enduring and successful 'not because of some deep cosmic truth, or any universal law of storytelling, but because it's the neatest way of showing deep character change' (2020: 5). Fictional stories do often leave their characters profoundly changed, whether through a radical reversal of circumstances, such as from wealth to poverty – which Aristotle called *peripeteia* and argued was a crucial component of tragic drama (Aristotle 1997: 61) – or through a character's internal shift of perception or understanding, which subtly alters their world. In this vein, writer Ursula Le Guin concludes that, at its heart, 'story is something moving, something happening, something or somebody changing' (2015: 123).

Characters are central to almost all fictional stories – even if they are not likeable, their motivations and experiences draw audiences in to vicariously experience a story world and the events in it. A fictional character (in traditional Western fiction) is likely to face conflicts in the course of a story (the 'difficult situations' Lightman refers to), culminating in a crisis or climax. Here, the character is often presented with a choice or decision. Robert McKee (recalling Iris Murdoch's characterisation of literature as 'close dangerous play') states that 'the crisis must be a true dilemma – the choice between irreconcilable goods, the lesser of two evils, or the two at once that places the protagonist under the maximum pressure of his life' (McKee 1997: 304). Consequently, characters' choices and actions frequently show us the meaning and theme of a story, and reveal something about those protagonists – as Will Storr puts it: 'If there's a single secret to storytelling then I believe it's this. *Who is this person*? Or, from the perspective of the character, *Who am I*? It's the definition of drama. It is its electricity, its heartbeat, its fire' (2020: 108, emphasis in original).

Fictional stories might also be distinguished by their *style*. This does not necessarily mean ornate and poetic prose – as Richard Phillips and Helen Kara remark, creative writing is not simply defined by its use of 'flowery language … and a surplus of adjectives' (2021: 41). Certainly, many effective works of fiction employ unadorned or minimalist prose. Nevertheless, audiences of fictional works may expect a richness of expression which stands in contrast to more 'functional' communication. For instance, Ursula Le Guin encourages writers to pay attention to the 'beauty' of fictional language, noting that 'a story is made out of language, and language can and does express delight in itself just as music does' (2015: 2). (Such aesthetic 'delight' in a medium might equally, of course, be found in visual storytelling.) In much Western or Euro-American fiction, there may also be an emphasis on indirectly 'showing' ideas rather than explicitly 'telling' information. For instance, prose descriptions might capture the spirit of the aphorism attributed to Anton Chekhov: 'Don't tell me the moon is shining, show me the glint of light on broken glass', while in all fictional forms, characters' personalities might be suggested through their actions or speech rather than described directly (for example, Gardner 1991).

In such ways, fiction creates and depicts a setting, and builds a fictional world, into which the reader or audience is immersed, vicariously entering the lives of the characters who inhabit it. (We return to these elements of fictional stories in Chapter 5, where we also explore the role of other aspects of fiction such as dialogue and point of view.)

These components of fiction should not be seen as prescriptive rules – works of fiction may play with, reinterpret or recast some or all of these elements (although in such cases, authors are often *consciously* breaking with tradition to create innovative stories, for example, McKee 1997: 54). And, of course, these elements will be used in distinctive ways in different fictional media – for example, a graphic novel builds a fictional world through its combination of visual and linguistic elements, whereas a short story can include passages of descriptive prose. However, we suggest that these ideas are useful starting points for thinking about how works of fiction tell compelling stories which resonate with readers or audiences.

> **Further reading: stories and fiction**
>
> Many resources exist for researchers interested in storytelling and fiction. Both *The Writer's Journey* (Vogler 2007) and *The Science of Storytelling* (Storr 2020) comprehensively analyse story structure, while Salesses (2021) offers a counterpoint to some dominant ideas about stories by also exploring non-Western literary traditions.
>
> A number of established authors have published insightful writing guides and/or memoirs which present practical information about craft and technique alongside personal reflections on the possibilities and purposes of fiction – examples include Ursula Le Guin's *Steering the Craft* (2015), Stephen King's *On Writing* (2010) and Anne Lamott's *Bird by Bird* (2019). (We list some further resources on fictional craft in Chapter 3.)

Fact and fiction

Fictional works often include some of these structural and stylistic elements, but, as we noted earlier, fiction can also be defined as stories about *imagined* characters and events. Certainly, it is often the case that in fiction, protagonists and their experiences, and the worlds they inhabit are overtly 'made-up' by an author, and readers understand that these stories are not supposed to represent 'real life' – something perhaps particularly evident in genres such as fantasy or science fiction. However, in some instances, the degree to which fictional characters and events are 'imagined' is more complex. For example, fictional works and characters may well draw from the author's own experiences or from real-life events. Notably, in the popular genre of 'biofiction' (Lackey 2016), fiction-writers construct a story based on a real person, such as a historical figure, combining biographical facts with fictional elements (writers might imagine details of the character's daily life, or sometimes create much more fantastical stories, as in Alan Lightman's novel *Einstein's Dreams*).

It is also the case that *other* forms of creative writing employ many (if not all) of the structural and stylistic elements of fiction discussed here without describing themselves *as fiction*. Creative non-fictional prose, memoirs and audio-visual documentaries often use a literary prose style (or the visual equivalent), may focus on characters undergoing change, or utilise traditional story structures, while also asserting that the events they depict are *true* (for example, Bricklebank 2006).

The genres of biofiction and creative non-fiction both underline how the status of any particular work as fictional (or not) depends, to some extent, on the claims an author (as well as publishers, booksellers and librarians) makes about it. As Patricia Leavy notes, drawing on the work of literary theorist Wolfgang Iser, one defining aspect of a work of fiction is that a text 'discloses its fictional nature' (Leavy 2022: 11). Similarly, narrative theorist Dorrit Cohn (1999) discusses how various 'signposts' serve to demarcate and distinguish fiction from non-fiction, while Richardson and St. Pierre point out that an author can choose how and whether to 'declare' that their work is fictional (2005: 961). Such signposts and declarations can be both explicit and implicit (such as through the marketing of a book, or its position in a library or book shop, the use of an invented character's name in a first-person narrative, or the author's use of an omniscient viewpoint), and may also rely on the use of the structural/stylistic elements discussed. Where a work employs these elements, there is arguably an assumption that it is 'made up' unless explicitly stated otherwise (as is usually the case in creative non-fiction or biofiction).

Of course, along with creative non-fiction writers, many academic researchers also employ creative-writing techniques (for example, Phillips and Kara 2021: 8), without necessarily declaring their work *is* a piece of fiction. Our focus in the following chapters is mainly on research-based work which does (in some way) make declarations about its own fictionality (although many of the points we discuss would also be of interest to researchers wishing simply to employ fictional techniques in their work). However, for now we note that non-fictional academic writing might well entail the use of lyrical prose, or, for instance, the vivid characterisation of individuals in fieldwork accounts. Fictional forms might even inform the structure of academic works – including, aptly, this book.

Navigating this book

In structuring our exploration of fiction and research in this book, we have drawn inspiration from the hero's journey.

Like Storr, we do not think that the hero's journey structure accesses a 'deep cosmic truth', but we do suggest that recognisable story forms can be thought-provoking and 'good to think with' – that they might resonate, inspire and suggest connections.

Accordingly, this chapter represents the 'call to adventure', drawing researchers out of their 'ordinary world' towards fiction. In Chapters 2 and 3, we introduce more potential 'mentors' and 'allies' to guide the heroic researcher on their way – theorists, writers and researchers whose work might offer insights, wisdom and guidance. In Chapter 4, we raise some 'difficult questions' about the use of fiction in research – which, like the 'innermost cave', represent challenges and tests to be overcome. Finally, in Part III (Chapters 5 and 6), we offer ideas about creating and sharing fictions, which might provide researchers with an 'elixir', enabling them to take their fictional discoveries back to their ordinary world!

Concluding thoughts

In this chapter, we have begun to trace points of contact between the practices of research and fiction, opening up ways to think about how they might connect and to consider how fiction may be useful to, or inform, research. We have highlighted how incorporating 'fiction' into research might involve fictionalisation, fictional thinking and/or works of fiction. We have explored how works of fiction frequently entail the selective use of structural and stylistic elements. While fiction often involves stories of imagined events and characters, underlying this aspect of fiction is an awareness that this is (at least partly) based on authorial declarations and other explicit/implicit framings of the text. In the following chapter, we delve deeper into these issues and explore in more detail how researchers have argued for the relevance of fiction from a range of theoretical and disciplinary vantage points.

> **Reflective questions**
>
> - Is there a history of fiction in your area or discipline?
> - Do you ever tell stories conversationally about your research?
> - Is your research topic or discipline represented in popular fictions, such as films, plays or prose? How do these popular fictions relate to your experience as a researcher and/or to your data?

> **Reflective exercises**
>
> 1. Fiction writers' reflections on storytelling and fictional craft can provide useful and thought-provoking insights for researchers embarking on fiction-related projects. Find an interview or essay in which a writer or artist discusses their fiction. Pay attention to what they think fiction is for and what it can do. Does their work raise questions about the relationship between fact and fiction? What do they think makes a successful story or work of fiction? Are there any parallels with your own work, or your goals for using fiction?
>
> 2. Ask your research colleagues or stakeholders about a work (or works) of fiction which have impacted them. Which

works of fiction are meaningful to them and why? Are there fictions which have changed their perceptions or beliefs, enabled them to think in new ways, or which chime with their own experiences? Are there stories, characters, events or even phrases from fictional works which have resonated with them? Articulating the subtle, personal and complex ways that fiction matters to people may help you refine your own goals for using fiction in your research.

2

Theoretical approaches to fiction and research

This chapter:

- Explores three rationales, and their theoretical underpinnings, for combining research and fiction:
  - Stories as fundamental to human experience.
  - The use of fiction to more fully and fairly represent human experience, sometimes problematising notions of truth or authority.
  - Fiction as a means of speculating or imagining alternative or future possibilities.
- Argues that researchers' rationales for the use of fiction are closely linked to their ontological and epistemological positioning.

Introduction

In this chapter we explore how researchers in various disciplines have argued for the use of fiction in research. Their rationales typically include practical, theoretical and/or ethical reasons and we identify three broad, often overlapping, themes therein:

1. the fundamental appeal of stories;
2. fiction's potential in relation to the politics of representation; and
3. fiction as a way to go beyond research data through speculating or imagining.

We show how rationales for using fiction are informed by key disciplinary (and cross-disciplinary) debates and paradigm-shifts (Kuhn 1970). We hope that readers will find ideas that resonate with their own disciplinary approach, but perhaps also explore new ways of thinking about the potential of fiction.

Common to many researchers' interests in fiction is the potential for *engagement*. As we will explore, what exactly 'engagement' means varies between researchers: fiction might engage audiences and/or participants because it is emotional, accessible, familiar, entertaining, surprising, life-like, challenging, amusing, disturbing, utopian or impossible (or any combination of these). Fiction's ability to engage is often contrasted with 'dry' academic or scientific writing and highly valued by researchers wishing to connect with audiences outside of specialist or academic circles, including via interdisciplinary and/or public engagement work (see Richardson and St. Pierre 2005; Gibson 2021; Leavy 2022). Such possibilities may appeal to many researchers, since engagement with wider publics is increasingly expected in the context of the so-called 'impact agenda' and associated performance measures (see Smith et al 2020). Ash Watson (2016) for example, makes the case for novel writing as a promising method for achieving the goals of 'public sociology' (Burawoy 2005). For other researchers, fiction is understood as a method to engage participants. Fictional methods may be used as part of participatory or co-production research designs and are sometimes viewed as more inclusive of marginalised or vulnerable participants, such as children, those from disadvantaged backgrounds or living with chronic illness (see Nägele et al 2018; Satchwell et al 2020) (but see also Chapter 4 for a critique of this assumption). Regardless of their particular motivations, most researchers employing fiction agree that it offers a *distinctive* means of communicating and thinking which stands apart from conventional research methods and writing, as we discuss in more detail now.

The pull of fiction: the fundamental appeal of stories

Across various disciplines, those who combine research and fiction often argue that there is something fundamentally human about stories. People make sense of their experience through both creating and responding to narratives, in ways which bring coherence, intelligibility and meaning to the ordinary chaos of life (Polkinghorne 1988).

Will Storr accounts for the power of fictional stories through evolutionary psychology. For instance, just as our brains respond involuntarily to changes in our environment because such changes might indicate imminent danger, so too do compelling stories hinge on moments of change 'that seize the attention of … protagonists and, by extension, their readers and viewers' (2020: 13). Storr also argues that the universal human social practice of sharing news and passing moral evaluations is exactly what is at play when people tell fictional stories (which likewise deal in the expression of shared morality, triggering our outrage if protagonists are unjustly treated, or bringing satisfaction when we see a protagonist make a commendable decision) – he concludes: 'the surprising discovery that's been waiting for us, at the destination of our long journey into our evolutionary past, is that all story is gossip' (2020: 143). The idea that stories – *in all forms* – are buried deep in our evolutionary makeup is echoed by many others: Augusto Boal asserts that 'theatre is the first human invention' (Boal 1995: 13), and comics writer and theorist Nick Sousanis observes the first human stories appeared in cave paintings – these visual narratives 'a means of grappling with experience before we had names for it' (2015: 60).

This human 'readiness or predisposition to organise experience into a narrative form' (Bruner 2002: 45) is evident in very young children, who routinely seek explanations for anomalous events, account for their own and others' intentions and actions, and recount what happened and how they feel about it (2002: 90). Meanwhile, neuropsychological research on 'mirror neurons' has shown how human brain cells are activated when people see someone else doing a physical action: the observer's brain shows a pattern of activity that would be expected if they themselves were performing the observed task (Gallese and Wojciehowski 2011). Such responses are found in other primates, suggesting a common evolutionary history to this social stimulation. And, as Gallese and Wojciehowski (2011) have found, reading *fictional* stories appears also to activate mirror neurons – generating what they call a 'feeling of body' as the reader vicariously experiences the life of a fictional character. Humans seem, then, to respond to stories – including fictional ones – in profound, involuntarily ways.

As Gallese and Wojciehowski's work suggests, the human drive towards stories can be understood as simultaneously individual and social. Social psychologists and sociologists have also explored this interplay, noting how stories bond societies, how people use narratives to make sense of their actions, account for their lives or construct their 'selves' (for example, Riessman 1993; Holstein and Gubrium 2000; Bruner 2002). Although stories often concern people's individual lives, stories also inevitably draw on culturally specific narratives about ageing and youth (Plummer 2001: 190–192), decline in old age (Gergen and Gergen 1988) or gendered expectations of mothers (May 2008), for instance. Although these narratives may be presented as non-fictional, frequently they depict life in ways which are familiar from literature, emphasising 'epiphanies' or turning points (Riessman 1993; Denzin 1997), 'hitting bottom' and recovering (Holstein and Gubrium 2000: 120–123) or triumphant stories of 'overcoming hurdles' (Plummer 2001: 195), so that it might even be claimed (as Jerome Bruner asserts) that [our experience of] 'life imitates art' (Bruner 2002: 121). From such perspectives, stories (including fictional stories) can be seen to play a central role in human experience and understanding.

In some cultures and groups, storytelling's role in making sense of the world may be particularly important or explicitly acknowledged. For First Nations peoples, and other North American Indigenous cultures, 'storytelling and knowledge are often one and the same' (Christensen 2012: 233). Such storytelling is often communal, collaborative and interactive. Similarly, African oral traditional storytelling (a practice which, although not universal or homogeneous, is found across many African societies), uses folktales, riddles and stories to transmit wisdom and impart moral lessons through collaborative telling, including through the conversational gatherings known as 'fireside chat' (Osei-Tutu 2023). And Patricia Hill Collins (2014) observes that through stories, African-American women in the US have long shared wisdom and found possibilities for resisting oppression in the context of a wider society which has silenced and disregarded their voices. She suggests that fiction – in the form of literature and narrative songs – is one of several 'important locations for constructing a Black feminist consciousness' whereby Black women articulate their 'subjugated knowledge' (2014: 251–252).

Stories, including fictional ones, can draw us in and affect us deeply, and for researchers who are part of, or engaged with, communities where storytelling carries a particular freight and significance, fiction may be a means to communicate with those groups in resonant and meaningful ways. For many researchers, then – whether they foreground biological, evolutionary, social or cultural perspectives – using fiction to explore, reflect on or share knowledge about the world capitalises on the uniquely human power of stories.

Addressing the politics of representation through fiction

Fuller and fairer representations

The social sciences – particularly qualitative research – have been the site of much innovation regarding fiction. Across a range of disciplines, researchers have argued that fiction can be a way to better, or more fully, represent social life.

Qualitative social researchers often wish to explore the meaning and complexity of lived experiences, convey closely observed interpretive 'thick descriptions' of social life (Geertz 2017), interrogate taken-for-granted truths and make the familiar strange (for example, Mason 2002). Fictional stories lend themselves readily to such aims. As we have noted, a tradition of anthropological fiction has harnessed fiction as a way to tell rich, layered and humanistic stories about cultures and the people in them (Schmidt 1984). The interdisciplinary practice of 'arts based research' has similarly embraced fiction (alongside dance, theatre, poetry and visual arts) as a means of inquiry, noting the affinities between the two forms, wherein artistic expressions can be seen as a 'species of qualitative research' (Barone and Eisner 2012: 46). And Patricia Leavy notes that for qualitative researchers, writing fiction is in many ways a 'natural extension' of what those researchers already do (2013: 20).

To varying degrees, qualitative researchers query some of the Enlightenment thinking we mentioned in Chapter 1, for instance, resisting binaries which assume research should be removed or objective rather than personal, engaged, emotional or embodied. Qualitative researchers often recognise, and are interested in exploring, the subjective and positional character of participants' experiences of the world, as well as their own active role, as researchers, in (re)constructing those experiences as research findings. Here, again, fiction offers a way to engage with such concerns.

For example, for researchers who are interested in the embodied nature of lived experience, or whose work seeks to query the boundary between mind and body, fiction can be a way to convey the 'essentially emotive, corporeal and intersubjective, visceral, sentient nature of our being' (Inckle 2010: 35; see also Christensen 2012). And although evocative *prose* offers one way to attend to corporeality, dramatic performances offer another particularly potent means of exploring and approaching embodied experience (for example, Raynor 2019) – since, as Augusto Boal remarks, the 'most important element of theatre is the human body' (2002: 16).

Fictional writing can also foreground emotions – perhaps challenging binaries of rationality/affect and objectivity/positionality, and validating the important role of emotions in the development of knowledge (Richardson 1997b; Inckle 2010). Through fiction, researchers might tell more emotive stories, which might affect a *reader* emotionally, convey the emotional experiences of *participants* and/or depict emotional aspects of the *research process* itself (Richardson 1997a; Inckle 2010; Christensen 2012; Hecht 2017).

The desire to tell emotive stories is often enmeshed with an intention to create empathetic representations of research participants which 'do justice' to their experiences and perhaps prompt change. Leavy, a pioneering figure in the use of fiction within research, has written extensively about such issues. As Leavy (2013) explains, research which *affectively* moves its audience is more likely to be *effective* in promoting change. Christensen similarly (2012) discusses how fictionalised research can help us to get under characters' (and thus participants') skin and experience some sense of how the world appears through their eyes. (And Patricia Leavy also notes that the distance fiction affords might mean readers are even *more* open-minded and empathetic towards a fictional character than a real person [Leavy 2022: 13].) Affecting fictional accounts are supported by depictions of what Leavy (2022: 13) calls a character's 'interiority' – their motivations, feelings, hopes and thoughts. Through the inclusion of sensory details and the conjuring of atmosphere (see also Chapter 5), well-told stories achieve 'verisimilitude' (Leavy 2013, 2022; Gibson 2021), such that the reader or audience members feel as though they are 'really there' alongside a character. When done well, people may feel they have been transported to geographically or temporally distant worlds which may be very different from their own (for example, Leavy 2013: 26–30; Helden and Witcher 2020). Consequently, the power of stories can help to make the case for legal or policy change, move individuals or groups to take political action, or inspire people to reconsider how they interact with others in their work or everyday life. Fiction's ability to invoke emotion and empathy, then, might support a researcher's broader social justice aims and/or constitute a way to enact reciprocity in their relationship to research participants and stakeholders, through generating impact which benefits the communities who are the focus of research (Inckle 2010; Leavy 2013).

The evocation of empathy in fiction is also closely linked to an appreciation of a character's *circumstances*. Ash Watson writes about how fictions (particularly novels) speak directly to the sociological concern of connecting selves and society – what C. Wright Mills termed 'the sociological imagination' (Watson 2016: 438; see also Bruce 2019; Leavy 2022: 14). Here again, fiction offers much potential: a novel can plunge readers into the lived experience of a single individual, while at the same time illuminating the social context of the character's life. For Watson, this 'panoramic' view provides 'a realistic experience of being in the social world through which interlocutors begin to see the themes and issues sociology is concerned with' (2016: 440). Similarly, Martha Nussbaum (2007) argues that the 'literary imagination' should be integral to both economic and legal scholarship (and public discourse more generally). She notes that novels bring readers into a uniquely intimate proximity with characters, but also allow space to *reflect* on the story: 'we might feel empathy with the plight of the characters, experiencing what happens to them as if from their point of view' while at the same maintaining 'a spectatorial judgment that the characters' misfortunes are indeed serious and have arisen not through their fault' (2007: 66). Understanding the ways in which characters are constrained, limited and treated unfairly can, perhaps, lead the reader to experience a meaningful empathy and reflect on how their own life relates to the character's, as well as gain a deeper understanding of wider social forces.

In these ways, researchers use fiction with the aim of telling 'fuller', 'richer' and perhaps also 'fairer' stories, in ways which make a difference in the world. The practical and ethical points discussed so far are pertinent to many qualitative researchers – regardless of their theoretical positioning. However, for some researchers, it is specifically *epistemic* questions and issues which are the driving force behind a turn to fiction, as we explore in the following section.

Problematising truth and authority

Some researchers (including some cited earlier in this chapter) have advocated for the use of fiction as a response to questions raised by post-structuralism, post-modernism, post-colonialism and (Black) feminist critiques of positivist epistemologies. For instance, post-structuralist theorists have argued that reality cannot exist independently from the language we use to discuss that reality (Derrida and Spivak 1976; Foucault 1998; and see Richardson 1997b). Similarly, post-modernist writers have called attention to the impossibility of creating meta-narratives that tell an overarching 'truth', instead emphasising fragmentation, multiplicity and uncertainty in the contemporary world and our own identities (Lyotard 1984). As Laurel Richardson explains, 'at the core of postmodernism is the doubt that any method or theory, discourse or genre, tradition or novelty, has a universal and general claim as the "right" or the privileged form of authoritative knowledge' (Richardson and St. Pierre 2005: 961). Post-colonial theorists have explored how Western scholarship has constructed, defined and 'Othered' non-Western cultures (for example, Said 1994). Feminists, in particular Black feminist and feminist Science and Technology Studies theorists, also highlight the power relationships in which all knowledge claims are embedded. Sandra Harding (1993), for example, alerts us to the situated character of all knowledge production. She disputes claims that research can be conducted from a 'neutral' standpoint and argues that the researcher's position, within gendered, racialised, classed, geographical, and so on hierarchies, inevitably shapes the production of knowledge, including the questions that are deemed worthy of asking and valid methods for answering them. All knowledge has this situated character but some subject positions and organisations, notably those with privilege, power and resources, are more able to obscure the contextual conditions of their knowledge production and thus endow their knowledge with the appearance of being 'from nowhere' (Haraway 1988; Nadar 2014). In *Black Feminist Thought*, Patricia Hill Collins powerfully demonstrates how ways of knowing, developed by Black women in the context of interlocking oppressions, are subjugated by those institutions which validate knowledge and the Eurocentric epistemologies they rely on.

Some writers in this tradition draw explicit links between research and the concept of fiction. For instance, Hayden White notes that the writing of history is a fundamentally literary endeavour, and argues that historians have used the 'archetypal story forms' (2000: 8) of tragedy, comedy, satire, romance (or heroic quest) to construct fictions about the past. A similar argument is made by the contributors to *Writing Culture* (Clifford and Marcus 1986) – a landmark collection of anthropological essays informed by post-structural and post-colonial insights. *Writing Culture*'s contributors argue that ethnographic texts are inevitably embedded within power relations, rely on rhetorical techniques, and are crafted through selective inclusions and omissions. As Clifford and Marcus observe:

> ethnographic writings can properly be called fictions in the sense of 'something made or fashioned', the principal burden of the word's Latin root, *fingere*. But it is important to preserve the meaning not merely of making, but also of making up, of inventing things not actually real. (*Fingere* in some of its uses, implied a degree of falsehood.) (1986: 6)

Such work has contributed to what has been called the 'crisis of representation' (for example, Denzin 1997) in the social sciences – the question of how researchers can and should write about culture, and what claims they can make about their authority and knowledge. For many, engaging with *fiction* offers some solutions to such questions.

Centrally, these theories open up the possibility of writing in new ways. Many researchers in this tradition do not seek to 'faithfully' depict reality, or to capture research participants' 'authentic natures and essential voices and then represent them in rich thick description' (Richardson and St. Pierre 2005: 969), or to unproblematically convey the voices of participants (Mazzei and Jackson 2012; Facca et al 2020). Instead, they may frame their writing in other terms, perhaps as 'creating a connection with' the research (Rhodes and Brown 2005: 482) or acting as a 'metaphor' for the topic of study (Rabbiosi and Vanolo 2017: 271). Such ideas open up the possibility of writing *fictionally* as a way to approach a topic without making straightforward truth claims about that writing. And, as some researchers note, if we accept that representations are always already 'fictional', declaring a piece of research to be 'fiction' might simply be a more honest way to represent it (for example, Rhodes and Brown 2005; Vickers 2010: 562).

Fiction can also be a powerful way to query writerly authority. For instance, fictional stories can *evoke* rather than *explain* the emotional complexity of a world (for example, Penfold-Mounce et al 2011). As Ash Watson argues, in contrast to the 'mimetic' communication of traditional research reports (which convey facts and information), fictional writing offers the potential for 'sympraxis' which is 'energetic, emotive, involving and creatively engaged' (Watson 2016: 437) – through fiction, a writer is no longer claiming authority over the data and its interpretation, and readers are invited to draw their *own* conclusions. Whereas 'traditional' research accounts may seem to fix and define reality, fictional texts and stories which make no such claims might avoid limiting and oppressing individuals or communities through the 'violence' of representation (Inckle 2010: 29; see also Nadar 2014; Raynor 2019: 9).

Reading a piece of 'fiction' invites the reader to bracket ideas of truth, falsity and authority; as Richardson and St. Pierre note, 'declaring that one's work is fiction is a different rhetorical move than declaring that one's work is social science' (2005: 961). Accordingly, instead of seeking to create texts which represent 'the truth', fiction can be a way to acknowledge and explore the inevitable partiality of any viewpoint, and the value of that knowledge. As Richardson and St. Pierre observe, 'having a partial, local, and historical knowledge is still knowing' (2005: 961), and similarly, Clifford and Marcus call for 'a cultural poetics that is an interplay of voices, of positioned utterances' (1986: 12). Fiction is well-placed to explore the limits and possibilities of such partial and various knowledge. Polyvocal fiction − representing many voices, none of which claim ultimate authority − might be a way to acknowledge that there are 'only multiple worlds and multiple representations of it' (Denzin 1997: 23; see also Banks and Banks 1998). And fiction's distinctive method of communication can leave space for multiple readings and interpretations of a text, undermining the idea that it is possible to present a 'view from nowhere' (Richardson 1997a: 3). For writers who wish to present ideas which are intentionally ambiguous and/or morally complex, fiction can be an ideal way to do this (for example, Banks and Banks 1998; Diversi 1998; Frank 2000; Inckle 2007).

Beyond data: imagination, speculation and future possibilities

In this final section, we identify a theme common to many researchers' use of fiction − the potential for fiction to tell stories which stand in contrast to what is already known, or what is empirical or real. Here, the character of fiction (as discussed in Chapter 1) as that which is *untrue or imagined* is foregrounded. This desire may stem from various practical, ethical or theoretical concerns (and in many cases overlaps with points we have discussed).

One such use of fiction, as we noted in Chapter 1, is the standard practice of anonymising social research participants' words − a subtle form of fictionalisation which distances research accounts from real individuals. However, some researchers also create entire fictional stories (for instance, using composite characters) in order to protect identities where a participant's unique circumstances or words could render their experiences recognisable even if a pseudonym were used (Douglas and Carless 2009; Markham 2012; Humphrey 2023). In a similar vein, social researchers sometimes wish to write accounts which draw on knowledge acquired from outside the research encounter (perhaps gained through prior personal experiences). These accounts can be rich and insightful but are potentially problematic because they cannot be presented straightforwardly as 'research findings'. However, creating a piece which is declared to be *fictional* can give a researcher freedom to incorporate this kind of peripheral and personal knowledge (Inckle 2010; Vickers 2010; Leavy 2013, 2022; Bruce 2019). In both these instances, fiction allows researchers to attend to ethical and practical concerns through distancing a research output from accounts which claim to be entirely 'real'.

In some cases, researchers may use fiction because they wish to tell *imagined* stories. This overlaps with some of the concerns we have already explored – for instance, researchers using fiction to convey embodied or emotional experiences of research participants are likely to employ their imagination to craft such stories. In particular, scholars across the humanities have noted that imaginative fiction offers a means to research topics which are otherwise inscrutable or inaccessible. For instance, Helden and Witcher argue that fiction and archaeology share an 'analytic plane' (2020: 2) and point to the discipline's tradition of using fictional techniques and of engaging with fictional representations such as novels. Helden and Witcher highlight the 'centrality of the imagination in the study of the past', observing that 'archaeologists excavate material traces from the ground and generate vast amounts of data, but these must be transformed into information and knowledge through a fundamentally creative process' (2020: 2) – a process which resembles, and might entail, the invention of fictional stories. Sungju Park-Kang similarly advocates for the use of imaginative fiction in the study of international relations. Park-Kang observes that when data is 'not available or not trustworthy' (as is the case with secretive states such as North Korea), a researcher 'might need to be a detective' who works with limited information, and perhaps creates imagined, fictional stories to fill in gaps (Park-Kang 2015: 371–372). For Helden and Witcher and Park-Kang, imaginative fiction does not *substitute for* empirical data, but it can provide a useful tool to explore things that empirical data cannot provide. Similarly, in some situations, fiction allows researchers to explore topics and experiences which it is impossible to access through other means, or which *can only ever* be imagined. For instance, through fictional stories we might inhabit the consciousness of non-humans (Rautio 2022), experience the moment of death (Cohn 1999: 22), give voice to inanimate objects (Cahill 2010), witness the end of the world (Kang et al 2017), visit the afterlife (Park-Kang 2015; Vanolo 2016) or (as we will discuss) step into a future which does not yet exist.

As we have noted, fiction can be defined as that which is primarily invented or imagined. And even the most realist or life-like fiction is, by definition, also *not* real. The unreal nature of fiction matters: knowing a story is a fiction can mean that readers may experience it more intensely, more painfully or more pleasurably, than real life (for example, Nussbaum 2007: 5–6). Equally, humans frequently seek out fiction depicting events which would be horrifying or overwhelming in reality – stories of murder, abuse, suffering and death – bearable only because of the distance afforded by knowing they are fictions (for example, Storr 2020: 117). As Aristotle theorised, experiencing such tragic, dramatic stories can provide 'catharsis' for an audience – the safe and controlled 'purgation' of negative emotions such as pity and fear (Aristotle 1997: 10). From these perspectives, fiction is valuable precisely because it stands in contrast to real life.

Indeed, for some researchers, this *counterfactual* quality is central to fiction's appeal. For example, Brazilian theatre practitioner Augusto Boal (through his Theatre of the Oppressed) has been an influential force in arts-inspired research, participatory action research and applied theatre. Boal argues that theatre is a tool that can challenge oppression. His techniques include Invisible Theatre, where undercover actors portray a scenario (for example, sexual harassment or racist abuse) in public places such as streets, restaurants or subway stations. Passers-by are unaware the situation is fictitious, and often become unwitting protagonists in the unfolding story (Boal 2002). Boal coined the term 'spect-actors' to describe audiences who become both observers *and* protagonists in these interactive stories (2002: 15).

In Forum Theatre, participants act out oppressive situations they have encountered in real life, but also enact alternative ways of responding that could overcome the oppression (for example, Boal 2002: 243–244). Boal's techniques do not necessarily result in 'works of fiction' (although they might), but they do centre 'fictional thinking' – the proposal and exploration of different possibilities. These theatrical scenarios open up a gap between 'reality' and 'fiction', allowing participants to view reality anew, a process Boal calls 'metaxis' (2002: 214) – the state of being in-between two worlds. In this case, imagined stories do not simply 'purge' difficult feelings about real life and enable the audience to continue as before (as in Aristotelian catharsis), but rather they open up an opportunity for reality to be approached differently; for Boal, entering this fictional space can be a transformational encounter, the catalyst for change.

Another way of exploring the space between the imagined and the real is through the use of comedy, including parody or satire. Geographer Helen Cahill (2010: 170) suggests that while realist fiction can evoke empathy, genres such as parody and surrealism can play other roles, such as exposing illogicality or making an audience question what they thought to be true. In particular, satire – by representing ordinary life in an exaggerated, unrealistic manner – can allow a writer to, as Cate Watson puts it, 'point up the absurd that always lurks beneath what hegemonic discourse claims as the rational' (2011: 402). Ethnographer and comedian Kate Fox observes that comedy can reveal a 'gap between how the world is and how the world should be' (Fox, cited in Phillips and Kara 2021: 158). Similarly, for researchers working with drama, theatrical parodies can serve as a kind of 'carnival' – a cathartic 'safe space' where actors can represent real life in a hyperbolic, humorous way, thereby processing real-world issues and concerns (Gembus 2018). Again, comedic approaches to research might or might not entail producing full 'works of fiction', but they can offer a form of 'fictional thinking' – asking 'what if' things were different – and inviting an audience to weigh this fiction against what is already known.

Fiction also offers a uniquely powerful medium for researchers whose interests relate in some way to the future. For instance, social researchers who have examined the outcomes of particular situations can share those insights via fiction, allowing readers to imagine themselves into scenarios which they might face in the future – which was the case in our own collaboration, where we produced short fiction as a resource for prospective egg donors (Tipper and Gilman 2019, 2020, 2022). Researchers interested in how people make sense of everyday life have also explored participants' speculations about what *could* happen in an imagined future, thereby tracing cultural views of what is expected and possible (for example, Clarke et al 2019). Stories of fictional futures can be ordinary and conceivable (as in the two previous examples), but they can also be remarkable and fantastical, drawing on the genres of speculative and science fiction. In fact, science-fiction writer H.G. Wells (who was keenly interested in the nascent science of sociology) called on turn-of-the-century social researchers to focus their energies on such speculation. Addressing the Sociological Society in London, he declared that 'the creation of Utopias – and their exhaustive criticism – is the proper and distinctive method of sociology' (Wells 1906: 367). Such fictional, literary speculations, Wells wrote, would allow sociologists to imagine and design an 'Ideal State' (1906: 368). More recently, Donna Haraway – whose work traverses the boundaries of science, philosophy and feminism – has written of 'speculative fabulation': a 'mode of attention, a theory of history and a practice of worlding' (2016: 230), in which storytelling, speculative fiction, science fiction (and science fact) all play a role in articulating and reimagining more-than-human kinship and ways of being.

Researchers engaged in social justice movements have indeed found that the creation of fictional utopias – just as H.G. Wells suggested – can be a useful research practice. Such 'visionary fiction' (Imarisha et al 2015: 3) shows what radical changes are possible in the long term. But they can also 'aid us in identifying issues in the present and in imagining and enacting better alternatives in the *near* future' (Crockett Thomas 2022: 10, emphasis in original) – fiction, then, can become a tool for critical research concerned with social justice and reform. Notably, both Imarisha et al and Crockett Thomas draw inspiration from the work of Octavia Butler, an acclaimed writer of what is now known as Afrofuturism – science fiction by Black and African diaspora authors. Afrofuturist fiction incorporates speculative stories alongside traditional or historical Black and African stories, generating fictions which critically interrogate oppression and imagine possible futures (Yaszek 2006).

Future-oriented fictions might explore utopias, as well as neutral or undesirable futures, including dystopian visions of society. In particular, science, technology, engineering and mathematics researchers who wish to explore the sometimes difficult consequences of scientific advances or challenges might employ fiction to do so. For instance, the social implications of medical futures (such as epidemics and diseases) can be imagined and played out through fiction (for example, Nesta 2015). The emergent research practice of 'Design Fiction' (Bleecker 2009) is also inspired by science fiction and uses speculative scenarios and imagined objects to ask 'what if' questions about future technologies. Examples include a world where computers are present in all aspects of human life, or 3D printing machines which can produce human organs. Images, art installations, documentaries or stories depicting these designs are presented as 'conversation pieces, with the conversations being stories about the kinds of experiences and social rituals that might surround the designed object' (Bleecker 2009: 7). Even if such futures are unpleasant or impossible, thinking fictionally about them enables us to think about what *could* happen and how we might react to it, generating insights that can inform both the present and the future.

Concluding thoughts

In this chapter, we have examined some common, overlapping, themes underlying many researchers' interest in fiction: the fundamental appeal of stories; fiction's potential to tell different kinds of research accounts which might address the politics of representation; and fiction as a way to move beyond data through the use of speculation or imagination. We have also shown how researchers' rationales for using fiction are linked to their ontological and/or epistemological positions – that is to say their understandings of the way the world is and how knowledge about it can be developed. Disciplinary debates and developments, such as the so-called 'crisis of representation' as well as social movements, have thus, for some researchers, driven their use of stories. In addition, changing agendas within universities and funding bodies (for example, promotion of interdisciplinary working or the 'impact agenda' [see Smith et al 2020]) have also arguably enabled the growth of fictional approaches to research in recent decades.

However, even among researchers who share common disciplines, or epistemological assumptions and rationales for using fiction, how they put theory into practice can vary widely. In the next chapter, we explore and showcase this variety, through a selection of examples which collectively illustrate the diversity of what doing research-fiction (or creating research-based fiction) can mean in practice.[1]

Reflective questions

- Which of the three rationales we have outlined in this chapter most closely aligns with your own work or ambitions? (Your answer may well include more than one.)
- What is your relationship to any participants or stakeholder communities involved in or implicated by your research? How does this shape your aspirations for using fiction?
- How do you understand the status of the knowledge your research can produce? How does this shape your reasons for using fiction? How do you understand the (potential) status of fiction in your research?

Reflective exercises

1. Taking inspiration from researchers who use fiction to speculate about future possibilities, imagine that you are presenting about your research-fiction at a conference. Take ten minutes to write down the comments and questions you might receive from your audience (imagining some different characters in the audience

might help to get you started). What does this exercise tell you about the epistemic norms within your discipline (or your expectations of them)? Do your own assumptions differ from them?

2. Many scholars are drawn to fiction because of its potential to interrogate ideas about knowledge and authority, or to convey multiple truths. Whether or not you take this approach, exploring other (perhaps unexpected) voices can be a productive way to think fictionally about your own work. Write for ten minutes about your research or research topic, imagining the point of view of someone whose voice is not represented in your research: examples might include a member of the public reading about your research findings in a newspaper, a transcriptionist listening to your interviews, the reflections of a laboratory or research assistant, or the perspective of a person who was mentioned by an interviewee but whom you did not interview. What does this exercise tell you about who has authority to speak about your research topic? (For more information on polyvocal texts, see Chapter 5.)

PART II

Fiction in practice

3

Examples of fiction in practice

> This chapter:
>
> - Showcases the variety of ways in which different researchers have used fiction in practice.
>
> - Describes examples of research-fictions which use existing works of fiction to 'think with', those which use or create fictional texts or ideas with participants, and those where new fictional outputs are created by researchers or artists.
>
> - Includes case studies of a range of fictional formats and genres, including a theatre production, a graphic novel, short stories and a novel.
>
> - Suggests further reading for readers interested in making comics, creating theatre or dramatic performances, and writing fictional prose.

Introduction

In the preceding chapters, we have reviewed theoretical and practical reasons that might lead researchers to employ fiction in their work. In this chapter, we explore what the use of fiction in research might *look like* in practice, by highlighting a range of examples and discussing seven case studies in particular.

Our examples represent various substantive research topics and disciplines (although as we have noted, much of the innovation regarding fiction has taken place in the social sciences). The nature of the fictional work varies too: some researchers draw on published novels or television series, other projects produce new works of fiction (written by researchers, participants, commissioned writers, or some combination of these). Our selection is not comprehensive – many more excellent examples exist – but the pieces we discuss here are ones which have moved, inspired or intrigued us. We hope that readers will likewise find inspiration, perhaps from disciplines outside their own, or from fictional formats that are unfamiliar to them.

We have structured this chapter around three roles that fiction can play in research:

1. *Thinking with fiction*: researchers articulate, clarify or explore a research problem, or generate theory, often through engagement with existing works of fiction.
2. *Researching with participant-created fiction*: researchers invite participants to think fictionally or create fictional stories. These participant-created fictions might generate data which is formally analysed (alongside or in place of more traditional research data). In some cases, participant-created fictions become a research output which communicates participants' experiences or concerns to a wider audience.
3. *Communicating and sharing research with fiction*: researchers create or commission a fictional output to enable knowledge exchange. The fiction might represent or communicate a specific project's findings, or may draw on more general academic or theoretical ideas.

Some researchers' use of fiction sits neatly within one of these categories, but (as we will discuss) these categories are far from discrete. Frequently, research-fiction serves multiple purposes at once, and the use of fiction may change or evolve during the course of the research. Nevertheless, these categories provide a useful starting point for exploring some of the diverse ways that research can incorporate fiction.

Thinking with fiction

As we have discussed, the potential for fiction to capture 'truths' about social life, or to express the kinds of insights many researchers also seek, means that existing works of fiction often resonate with researchers and academics. This is evident in the use of published and popular works of fiction as a teaching resource.[1] Extracts from fictional works (often novels) sometimes also appear as epigraphs and quotations in academic work. In these instances, fictional extracts can serve to illustrate a theoretical concept, or to validate a researcher's conclusions, as Cate Watson wryly observes, 'appealing to the truths offered by fiction (as well as showing off the erudition of the researcher)' (2011: 398).

However, some researchers engage with fiction in a more sustained and exploratory manner — not only to illustrate ideas, echo findings or display erudition — but, more fundamentally, to 'think with'.[2] This kind of engagement with fiction can take many forms. For instance, sociologist Jennifer Mason draws on a range of literary works (including novels) alongside qualitative data to build her theory of 'affinities' — the multifaceted ways in which people create and experience relationships with others and with the world around them. She notes that creative writers often bring 'sensibilities of perception' (Mason 2018: 151) to bear on everyday experience, which enable them to capture fleeting, elusive sensations and associations that are 'simultaneously tangible and intangible' (2018: 65). Here, fiction's distinctive ability to enter into the shifting consciousness of a particular individual is one way to access the kind of embodied, subtle attention to everyday life which is central to Mason's theoretical project. Fiction, in this instance, seems to demonstrate both a *way of doing* social research and of *thinking theoretically* about social life.

In a similar vein, Ruth Penfold-Mounce et al (2011) draw inspiration from the fictional television series *The Wire*, which explores crime, policing, drug use and everyday life in Baltimore (and is itself the product of in-depth, participant research by its creators David Simon, a former journalist, and Ed Burns, a former detective and school teacher). Penfold-Mounce et al argue that *The Wire* — with its complex, multiple, overlapping, sometimes-unfinished stories of the city of Baltimore and its people – exemplifies Andrew Abbott's call for a 'lyrical sociology' (2011: 162), which 'does not explain or comprehend. In fact, it confuses and mystifies, it complicates and subverts' (2011: 163). *The Wire* is, they argue, *already* a piece of 'sociological fiction', and through its multi-layered, evocative telling, provides a model for the practice of sociology.

In the field of economics, Martha Nussbaum (2007) argues that novels (one aspect of what she calls the 'literary imagination') provide a crucial resource to think with, enabling a reader to identify with characters while at the same time fostering an appreciation of the contours of social life and constraints on human action. Nussbaum uses a close reading of Charles Dickens' *Hard Times* to interrogate economic theories of rational choice and utilitarianism, so that this fictional story becomes one voice in a dialogue through which researchers might explore and construct social theory.

In various ways, the work of Mason, Nussbaum and Penfold-Mounce et al shows how fiction can serve not only to illustrate academic concepts or reiterate research findings. Instead, it might offer a way to think about the *practice* of research itself, and, just like empirical data, can play a central role in the generation, articulation or refinement of theories about social life.

While *The Wire* and *Hard Times* offer expansive narratives for researchers to engage with, thinking with fiction can also entail drawing on existing fictional *characters*. Deborah Netolicky (2019) found that the character of the Cheshire cat from Lewis Carroll's *Alice in Wonderland* books was a fruitful metaphor to explore senior teachers' ideas of best-practice leadership. The ambiguous cat – who is both present and absent, and who offers guidance without seeming to do so – allowed Netolicky to articulate and examine teachers' understandings of the subtle qualities of a 'good leader'.

Relatedly, Charlotte Wegener (2014) used the character Phineas from A.S. Byatt's novel *The Biographer's Tale* as an imagined interlocutor in order to reflect on her own research – thereby 'thinking with' fiction, while at the same time creating a *new* fictional dialogue. Similarly, Helen Kara (2013) wrote fictional conversations with an imagined being to explore questions about the practice of research (although in Kara's case, the fictional character was a 'PhD devil' of her own invention, not a character from an existing work). Both Wegener and Kara's imagined conversations show how researchers can incorporate fiction into their work, and also recall Elizabeth St. Pierre's discussion of creative writing as a means of *analysis* in itself:

> I used writing as a method of data analysis by using writing to think; that is, I wrote my way into particular spaces I could not have occupied by sorting data with a computer program or by analytic induction. ... I made accidental and fortuitous connections I could not foresee or control. ... *Thought happened in the writing.* (Richardson and St. Pierre 2005: 970, emphasis in original)

The kind of creative writing that Richardson and St. Pierre advocate, which embraces dreams, allusions and memories, is not necessarily *fictional* (although it might be). Nevertheless, their argument underlines the potential for fictional writing as a means for researchers to explore and discover insights, and perhaps analyse data (see also Frank 2000: 485–487; Phillips and Kara 2021: 125). In such instances, 'thinking with' fiction in research might occur not only through reading existing works, but in the *creation* of stories.

Works of fiction can also be used by researchers to open dialogues with participants – after all, people think about their own lives through storytelling, and often talk about popular fiction to make sense of their lives, evaluating the actions of fictional characters, and comparing their own lives against them (for example, Storr 2020). Sociologist Katherine Davies (2023), for example, used clips from *The Simpsons* in focus groups about young people's sibling relationships. Bart and Lisa's iconic relationship stimulated rich discussions of participants' own experiences and understandings of heredity, relatedness and the social construction of sibship. Similarly, Laura Bohannan – an anthropologist noted for her pioneering ethnographic novel, *Return to Laughter* (written under the pseudonym Elenore Smith Bowen) (Bowen 1964) – reflects on the potential of fiction to spark dialogue in her essay 'Shakespeare in the Bush' (1966). In the essay, Bohannan describes how she related the plot of *Hamlet* to a community of Tiv people in West Africa, with whom she was conducting fieldwork. The participants were intrigued by the story, and Bohannan's retelling of the play inspired a rich discussion with the community about morality, families, leadership, ghosts and the workings of the spiritual realm, as well as the nature of storytelling itself (recalling Osei-Tutu's [2023] analysis of traditional African oral storytelling as a means of collaborative knowledge creation). Such examples show how research participants (not only researchers) might use fiction to 'think with', inspiring discussions which offer valuable research insights.

Researching with participant-created fiction

Although researchers sometimes find inspiration in published works of fiction, a more common use of fiction in social research involves inviting participants to create stories. As we will explore, participant-generated fictions can take many forms, and they may appeal to researchers for different reasons.

'Story completion' is a method gaining traction among qualitative social psychologists. Here, respondents are presented with a 'story stem' – a line or two depicting a fictional character and a hypothetical scenario – and are invited to write a story in response, imagining what happens next. Story completion was initially used in psychoanalysis as a 'projective test' (akin to the Rorschach test) where responses are assumed to reveal 'unconscious "truths" about the story writers' (Clarke and Braun 2019: 100). However, for contemporary social psychologists working from a social constructionist perspective, respondents' stories offer a way of accessing *socio-cultural discourses*, revealing dominant ways of making sense of a topic. This method has been used to explore various substantive topics, including sexual relationships, weight management and eating disorders, and attitudes about physical appearance (Clarke et al 2019); we look in more detail at one such study in Box 3.1.

Story completion asks participants to imagine what could happen next. In a similar vein, many social researchers have found that asking participants to imagine future scenarios generates rich data. For instance, Kate North (2017) invited parents and carers of children with an Autism Spectrum diagnosis to write fictional stories based on the hero's journey story structure, where they imagined their own future, having overcome obstacles and problems. She identified recurring ideas in the stories and analysed

Box 3.1: Story completion as method: discourses about body hair and gender

In order to explore discourses surrounding male hair removal, Victoria Clarke and Virginia Braun (2019) used the story stem 'David has decided to start removing his body hair ...'

A story stem can take any form, although it is usually written in the third person, so that the respondent is 'situated outside the story' (Clarke and Braun 2019: 10). In addition, a 'contested idea' or 'cliff hanger' can encourage fulsome responses (Braun et al 2019). Clarke and Braun's stem in this case suggests a moment of *change* – it implies that something has triggered David to take this new course of action, inviting participants to respond with narratives that explain and explore this change.

Clarke and Braun found that participants' stories offered many insights into cultural discourses about masculinity and hair removal. For instance, the stories commonly depicted David as excessively hairy – in one story, David appeared in horror movies and was awarded the 'title of the world's hairiest man' (Clarke and Braun 2019: 104). The researchers note that hair removal can be seen as a feminising practice, but in these stories the 'construction of excess or abnormality ... provided a clear justification for removal that did not (necessarily) threaten David's masculinity' (Clarke and Braun 2019: 104).

Often, data generated through story completion tasks is analysed thematically (that is, stories are broken into distinct, recurring themes). However, in this case, Clarke and Braun examined the stories in their entirety, paying attention to their narrative structure – how they unfold and are presented in time, and the moral evaluations they employ (Clarke and Braun 2019: 101).

For Clarke and Braun, story completion offered a way to explore the narratives that people use to make sense of their worlds, and the ways that such understandings can be culturally bound and delineated (see also Chapter 2). As they also observe (reflecting on another study), stories, because they are not 'real', might also enable respondents to express

> controversial views they would not readily discuss in face-to-face interviews (Clarke et al 2019: 9).
>
> Story completion may also allow researchers to bridge the gap between positivist and qualitative methodologies, since the method can accommodate a comparative design: for instance, researchers can present respondents with the same hypothetical scenario but alter the gender of the fictional character (thus generating data about gendered expectations and discourses) or they could compare male and female respondents' stories (Clarke et al 2019: 7–8). However, Clarke and colleagues also note that qualitative researchers may need to consider how to interpret such data to avoid essentialising 'gender' or falling back on positivist assumptions.

them thematically. In a study of human relationships with animals, Paulina Rautio's research team (which included a famous science-fiction writer) asked young people in Finland to create fictions about future cities where humans were 'no longer the ruling species' (Rautio 2022). Young people responded enthusiastically to this prompt, creating worlds where, for instance, giant mice menaced humans. These speculative stories generated data about how human–animal relationships are currently understood, and how we might reimagine them.

These 'what if' stories, as we noted in Chapter 1, can be seen as a form of 'fictional thinking' even if they do not always generate 'works of fiction'. However, in some research, participants' speculations do also produce fictional works for wider consumption. For example, in the Prison Break research project, Phil Crockett Thomas used creative writing workshops with participants interested in transformative justice and 'prison abolition' – a movement which calls for alternatives to incarceration. Participants wrote short stories in order to 'imagine a future without exclusion and punishment' (2022: 7). Their stories explored speculative and science-fiction scenarios, such as virtual reality systems through which victims could vicariously punish their attackers, and a future world where prisons were repurposed into recreation centres. Unlike the fictions produced in story completion studies (which generate data later analysed by researchers), for Crockett Thomas, these stories were *both* part of the research process (wherein meanings were explored and expressed) *and* an output which brought these ideas directly into the public sphere.

Crockett Thomas' work also highlights how participant-created fiction is particularly attractive to participatory and action researchers who wish to engage participants. In our next example (Box 3.2), we explore another participatory project where fiction was both part of the research *process* and resulted in a *product* that could be shared more widely (for example, Phillips and Kara 2021: 114). In such cases, fiction might be the *means of generating data* but it might also be a way in which data is shared – blurring the boundary between fiction as data generation and as knowledge exchange.

Box 3.2: Stories2Connect – creating stories with young people

In the Stories2Connect project, social researchers Candice Satchwell and colleagues worked collaboratively with 65 disadvantaged young people who had experience of disability, of being in alternative care, or of being young carers (Satchwell et al 2020).

Since, as the researchers note, 'stories are central to our means of communicating with ourselves and one another' (2020: 875), the research used fictional story-making both to generate meanings *with* participants, and also to convey research findings to the public, including other similarly situated young people. The goal was to produce stories that might 'connect people and challenge stereotypes' (2020: 887).

Over three years, the group held meetings, creative workshops and interviews (conducted by both adult researchers and the young people themselves) – producing 48 fictional short stories, which are available as text and videos on the project's website.[3] Many of the stories are read aloud and accompanied by animations or illustrations. The stories on the website are aimed at children and young people who might identify with the issues explored. For Satchwell et al, these stories are a legitimate presentation of their collaborative research findings (2020: 885), although not the only possible one.

Some of the stories were created by the young people themselves (facilitated by an adult workshop leader); some were the product of a young person working one-on-one with an adult researcher; and some were written by adult researchers or fiction-writers inspired by interview data (2020: 882). All of the stories reflect the themes from the data and were 'tested out' (2020: 885) on young people, who offered feedback about whether they were convincing and representative of their experiences.

The stories explore everyday aspects of the young people's lives, including experiences of school, bullying, work, bereavement and disability. The stories often incorporate vivid and specific details from young people's ordinary lives, from special relationships with pets to 'unusual obsessions', such as – in one instance – a seemingly incongruous passion for housework and cocktails (2020: 883). Satchwell et al note that the inclusion of 'unusual narratives and details is exactly what makes these stories realistic' (2020: 883).

One story, 'Train Alone Day' (inspired by multiple interviews, but written and illustrated by an adult writer), follows teenaged Kerry who has been planning her first trip alone on public transport. However, Kerry's carefully laid plans are disrupted when, first, all the trains are cancelled, and then her phone fails:

> I was living a disaster; this wasn't in the script. The rule is that if anything big goes wrong, I phone [Dad]. We didn't talk about what I should do if my phone broke, or if it didn't work or if it ran out of battery. I suppose he didn't want to frighten me. I wanted to scream, cry and shout.

Kerry's troubles mount: at the station, she encounters her elderly neighbour, Mrs Bennett, who has become confused and disoriented on her journey

Figure 3.1: 'In the rain': scene from 'Train Alone Day'

Source: Art by Deborah Michel. Copyright © Stories2Connect project.

back from collecting her cat from the cattery. As well as dealing with her own problems, Kerry must now assist Mrs Bennett (Figure 3.1).

Kerry, like many other characters in these stories, is not labelled as 'disabled' or as having 'Special Educational Needs', but we sense that this series of small dramas is very challenging for her. This ambiguity exemplifies the authors' decision to leave 'deliberate gaps' (Satchwell et al 2020: 884) in the narrative where readers could fill in meanings for themselves, and also reflects the fact that for the young people, such diagnoses and labels did not define their identities; instead, the researchers aimed to create fictional characters whose 'idiosyncrasies, anxieties and triumphs' speak to their 'human characteristics rather than medical or psychological diagnoses' (Satchwell et al 2020: 885; see also Inckle 2010: 36).

Satchwell et al's work illustrates the power of collaborative storytelling – these fictions were crafted through engagements between participants, researchers and professional writers. This collaborative construction of fictions can allow participants to explore new ideas and refine them into a finished product, and also allow researchers to ask questions about and witness the process of story creation.

In another participatory fiction project, Larissa Nägele et al (2018) conducted research with people suffering from chronic infections. Utilising a 'Design Fiction' approach, Nägele et al asked participants to write short science-fiction stories about what their future medical treatment might look like. The researchers then worked collaboratively with participants to develop this sci-fi 'storyworld' through role-play and illustrated storyboards, and via the construction of a 'diegetic artefact' – an invented object from the fictional future. In this instance, the stories were analysed by researchers but also presented to stakeholders (in this case, medical manufacturers) as a fictional output of the research.

Satchwell et al's videos also demonstrate the potency of video as a means for sharing research-fictions – the animations and illustrations add depth and nuance to the stories. Similarly, in Nägele et al's Design Fiction, illustrated storyboards and creation of an imagined physical object were crucial parts of the fictional creation. Stories, in these cases, are not composed solely of written words. The significance of multidimensional, non-verbal storytelling is underlined by Caroline Lenette et al (2019), who worked collaboratively with refugee women in Australia to make 'digital stories' of the women's lives (which, although autobiographical, often employed fictional elements). In these videos, stories were enhanced by the resonance of a human voice reading the words aloud, the use of illustrations which included meaningful visual symbols, and the addition of music.

This potential for fiction to engage with the non-verbal (through physicality, images, music, voices and objects) is, of course, also central to dramatic work. For some researchers, participant-generated dramatic fiction may take the form of role-playing (often inspired by the work of Boal). In one project, geographer Helen Cahill (2010) drew on Forum Theatre to conduct participatory research in Vietnam and Australia, where workshop participants acted out scenarios related to sexual health in order to challenge dominant discourses and find solutions to real-life problems. The use of imaginative role play within theatrical workshops is well-established (for example, see also Gembus 2018; Conrad 2023). However, role-play can take other forms in research. For instance, although computer games remain a relatively untapped avenue for conducting social research, they also entail role-playing and immersion in fictional, socially complex scenarios, where people become protagonists in unfolding stories (for example, Castronova 2006). In one study, Kang et al (2017) drew on data from more than 80,000 individuals playing a computer game which depicted the end of the world. Kang's research team wanted to explore how humans might actually navigate the apocalypse and this simulation allowed them to analyse and observe how participants behaved in, and *enacted* the fictional story of, this imagined future.

Where dramatic or theatrical stories are generated with research participants, they do not necessarily result in public performances. However, performances of dramatic fictions *can* be a potent way to share research more widely. In some cases, research participants may co-create a fictional drama which is then also used to share the insights or findings. For instance, in collaboration with research participants in the north east of England, geographer Ruth Raynor co-created the fictional play *Diehard Gateshead*, which 'engaged with and made visible women's lived experiences in austerity'

(Raynor 2019: 3). The collaborative process itself generated insights for Raynor, and also offered a way to present the issues to a general audience. Similarly, Diane Conrad (2023) worked with a group of 'street-involved youth' in Canada to develop fictionalised performances that communicated their experiences and the challenges they faced. Conrad did not consider the young people's input 'data' as such – instead, her research framed the young people as 'experts engaged in knowledge production and action toward educating service providers' (2023: 365).

Communicating and sharing research through fiction

In the examples discussed so far, fiction has been embedded in the research process – employed or created in the course of data/theory generation. However, many researchers look to fiction *after* they have conducted research, with the aim of sharing findings in a fictional format (although, once again, we note that straightforward categories such as 'dissemination' and 'data generation' are often blurred). In the examples which follow, we focus on researchers who have sought to communicate research findings through fiction, specifically though drama, comics and written prose.

Communicating with dramatic fictions

As we have mentioned, theatrical performances are an effective way to communicate with wide audiences. While such performances can be co-created with participants, in some instances, researchers might employ a professional playwright in order to benefit from their skills (Saldaña 2005) – and our next case illustrates exactly this kind of research-practitioner collaboration (see Box 3.3).

Theatre has considerable potential to engage and affect audiences through live performances. Afterwards, a recording of the performance might be made available, but if a play is designed to be immersive or interactive, a recording is unlikely to replicate the impact of the original experience or capture its 'intimacy and humanity' (Saldaña 2005: 105). (For example, excerpts of *Passing On* are available online, although to appreciate the play in its entirety, it would be necessary to attend a live performance.) Film has the advantage of preserving a dramatic

Box 3.3: *Passing On*: verbatim theatre about end-of-life care

Passing On is a play produced through a collaboration between social researchers at the University of Warwick (led by Gillian Lewando Hundt), theatre director Claudette Bryanston and playwright Mike Kenny. Since 2011, it has been performed at various UK venues for audiences of medical and social care professionals, academics and the general public (Lewando Hundt et al 2019).

This piece of 'research-based theatre' is based on qualitative research with bereaved people, specifically people whose relatives died within 48 hours of admission to hospital. The script was developed through interactive workshops involving researchers and the creative team, and draws entirely on interview transcripts – an example of 'verbatim theatre'. Although verbatim theatre does not *necessarily* employ fictional techniques, in *Passing On*, participants' words were combined with theatrical devices and invented details to tell the story of two fictional characters, Joyce and Jim, an English Midlands couple who accompany Joyce's elderly mother to hospital, where Joyce's mother later passes away.

Passing On aims to explore complex questions which arise in end-of-life care. How do (and how should) professionals and families discuss or prepare for death? What is a 'good' death? Should dying patients know everything about their condition, or is it sometimes better if they remain unaware?

It is an immersive experience: on arrival, audience members are issued numbered tickets, as if they too are waiting to be admitted. And, throughout the play, actors portraying hospital staff address the audience directly, musing on their own role in the proceedings. Afterwards, audience members can remain and engage in a group discussion about the play and their own experiences. The team was inspired by Augusto Boal's Forum Theatre (performances which actively engage the audience and empower them to find solutions to real-life problems).

A striking element of the play is that the role of Joyce's ailing mother is performed by a life-sized puppet which the actors control (Figure 3.2).

Examples of fiction in practice

Figure 3.2: Actors Alison Belbin and Paul Nolan playing Joyce and Jim in a production of *Passing On*, along with the puppet which represented Joyce's mother

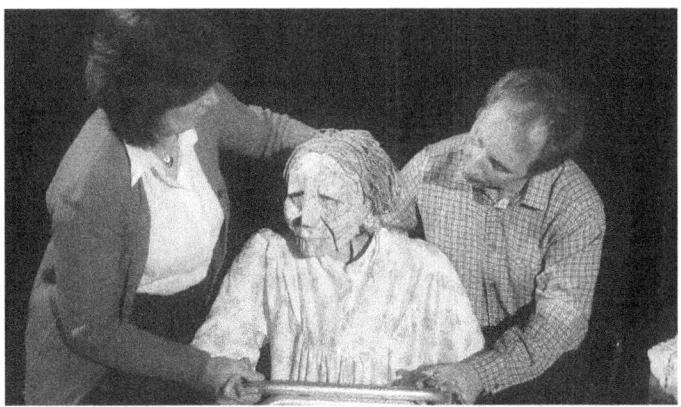

Source: Photo courtesy of STAMP Theatre and Media Productions CIC (formerly known as Santé Theatre).

The puppet was not intended to be naturalistic, although the team did ensure that its hands were particularly detailed, since holding a dying person's hands is often a significant aspect of end-of-life care (Bryanston and Lewando Hundt nd).

Although the puppet was not a 'real' person, actors and audience members found it both believable and moving. The puppet seems to straddle fictional and non-fictional worlds in a uniquely compelling way; as the team note, 'only a puppet can breathe its last breath on stage. The puppet enables the unplayable to be played. It can die' (STAMP nd). In this sense, fiction seems to create a (perhaps 'safe' or cathartic) space in which the audience might come close to the reality of death, and explore some of the difficult questions which surround it.

The play is, in part, an example of how research might be communicated through fiction. However, the researchers also transcribed and analysed the after-show discussions (Lewando Hundt et al 2019) – thereby using fiction to generate additional insights and data.

performance and making it accessible to more people, as well as creating the possibility for the action to be set in multiple locations and for actors' faces to be seen more clearly than is usually possibly in a theatre. However, film-making is costly, which is perhaps one reason it is less commonly used. One notable example is Kip Jones' collaboration with filmmaker Josh Appignanesi, which resulted in the fictional film *Rufus Stone*, based on Jones' qualitative research with older gay and lesbian people (Appignanesi 2012; Jones 2013).

> **Further reading: drama and theatrical fictions**
>
> For researchers interested in creating fictional drama, David Ball's *Backwards and Forwards* (1983) is a well-regarded guide to developing plays. Robert McKee's *Story* (1997) is a comprehensive introduction to both screenwriting and story structure. More specific resources also exist regarding Theatre of the Oppressed and Forum Theatre (Boal 1995, 2002); ethnodrama (Saldaña 2005); and verbatim theatre (Anderson 2007; Hammond and Steward 2012).

Passing On also highlights the possibilities of verbatim fictions. For researchers working with qualitative interviews, this can offer a way to produce an artistic representation of the data which remains 'faithful' to participants' actual words (although some researchers do problematise the idea that verbatim speech is a 'true' representation of participants' voices [Shah and Greer 2018]). As *Passing On* neatly illustrates, fictional or fictionalised elements can be used within verbatim pieces to craft an engaging story. In another example, social researcher Harvey Humphrey created a verbatim play about trans and intersex activism using transcripts of interviews with LGBTI people (Humphrey 2023). The play – entitled *AS IS* – is structured around a fictional scenario and incorporates a 'narrator' who introduces the audience to a range of activists. The fictionalised activists are composite characters, which provided anonymity for real interviewees who had spoken about sensitive issues.

Like *Passing On*, theatrical performances based on research often take the form of verbatim theatre – many other 'ethnodramas', which present social or ethnographic data, consist of verbatim content, fictionalised to various degrees (Saldaña 2005; Anderson 2007; Hammond and Steward 2012; Taylor et al 2017; Shah and Greer 2018). Aside from theatrical productions, interview transcripts (or other narrative data) can also generate verbatim poetry (for example, Mason 2018; Davis 2022). However, it is notable that verbatim fictional *prose* is less common, although Patricia Leavy's collection *Low Fat Love Stories* comprises 16 short fictionalised pieces which draw heavily on words from qualitative interviews (see Leavy 2022: 182–183).

Verbatim fiction, with its fidelity to data, can grant authority to a piece of fiction, and may allow participants to recognise themselves and their words in the story. However, some research-based fiction takes a different approach, creating fictions which (although informed by research insights) are entirely imagined, as is the case in our next case study – the graphic novel, *Lissa* (see Box 3.4).

Communicating with comics

Box 3.4: *Lissa*: **an ethnographic novel about medical decision-making**

Lissa is a graphic novel written by anthropologists Sherine Hamdy and Coleman Nye, with artwork by Sarula Bao and Caroline Brewer (2017). The story combines elements of Hamdy's research about kidney transplantation in Egypt and Nye's work on genetic testing and preventive surgery in the US. Its title is a colloquial Arabic word meaning 'there's still time'.

The novel follows two friends, Layla and Anna, as they each navigate medical dilemmas. Layla and her family are Egyptian; Anna is from the US but her family has been living in Egypt for several years when the story begins.

After Anna's mother dies of breast cancer, Anna is tested for the BRCA gene to determine whether she is also at heightened risk of the same disease. When the result is positive, she must decide whether to have a preventive mastectomy. Meanwhile, Layla's father is suffering with end-stage kidney disease, forcing the family to manage his care and debate the possibility of a kidney transplant. Most of the action takes place in Egypt and unfolds against the backdrop of the 2011 revolution.

Lissa's focus is on individual lives, but we glimpse, too, how wider social forces – US imperialism, political corruption, 'big pharma', environmental pollution, access to medical care, religious and cultural beliefs about bodies and medicine – play into Anna and Layla's decisions and experiences.

Some of the Egyptian characters' views about medical issues are informed by understandings of Islamic teachings. Radical medical interventions – in the form of organ transplants or preventive mastectomies – are resisted by some of the Muslim characters, at least partly for religious reasons. For instance, Layla asks Anna, 'Why would you mutilate yourself because of a disease you don't have?' (Hamdy and Nye 2017: 120). And although Layla and her brother offer to donate a kidney, Layla's father rejects this idea: 'No one is giving me a kidney. God in His Perfect Wisdom, created us whole. ... We cannot give away what is not ours to give' (2017: 110) (see Figure 3.3).

However, *Lissa* intentionally avoids presenting a simplistic binary of 'Muslim' versus 'Euro-American' beliefs about bodies and medicine, and seeks to offer a more subtle account (2017: 265). For example, Anna's father also tries to dissuade Anna from undergoing a preventive mastectomy, seeing the operation as an unnecessary mutilation of her currently healthy body. And, as the story progresses, it becomes clear that for *all* of the characters, seemingly personal decisions always entail other people and other bodies, since individual bodies are inevitably enmeshed in complex social relationships.

As comics writer Paul Karasik reflects in *Lissa*'s afterword, there is 'a certain type of visual resonance one can only feel with comics' where 'words collide with pictures and comics magic occurs' (Karasik 2017: 243). *Lissa*'s power lies not only in its storyline, but in the way it communicates that story visually, for example, the graphic representation of Anna's sense of isolation when her mother becomes ill (see Figure 3.4).

Figure 3.3: Layla's family grapples with the possibility of kidney donation

Figure 3.3: Layla's family grapples with the possibility of kidney donation (continued)

Source: Extract from the graphic novel *Lissa: a story about medical promise, friendship, and revolution* by Sherine Hamdy and Coleman Nye, illustrated by Caroline Brewer and Sarula Bao, University of Toronto Press (2017). Copyright © University of Toronto Press 2017. Reprinted with permission of the publisher.

Hamdy and Nye created *Lissa* in order to explore potential connections between their distinct research areas; Hamdy writes, 'We thought, "what would it be like to bring together two characters with a strong bond of friendship, each of whom has to make a life-and-death medical decision

Examples of fiction in practice

Figure 3.4: News of Anna's mother's diagnosis spreads at Anna's school

Source: Extract from the graphic novel *Lissa: a story about medical promise, friendship, and revolution* by Sherine Hamdy and Coleman Nye, illustrated by Caroline Brewer and Sarula Bao, University of Toronto Press (2017). Copyright © University of Toronto Press 2017. Reprinted with permission of the publisher.

that the other can't understand?" ' (2017: 265). While *Lissa* communicates findings from both anthropologists' research, it is not simply a piece of dissemination – instead, Hamdy and Nye have taken their research findings and *asked new questions* of that research, using fiction to speculate about imagined and possible stories and situations.

> **Further reading: making comics and graphic novels**
>
> For researchers who intend to work in this medium, Scott McCloud's *Understanding Comics* (1994) is an engaging guide to comics theory and production, which itself takes the form of a comic. Both Nick Sousanis (2015) and Juliet Fall (2021) also reflect (in graphic form) on using comics to explore academic ideas and theories. Specific insights into creating research-based comics can be found in Hamdy and Nye's appendices (2017) and in McNicol (2019), who also discusses the use of software for generating comics art.

In *Lissa*, complex anthropological ideas are made engaging and accessible to a wide audience through the 'proudly pulp' form of comics (Hamdy and Nye 2017: 13). Other researchers have also found that comics offer a uniquely engaging method of communication. Sarah McNicol (2019) created comics with Asian women in the UK to tell autobiographical stories (which often muddied the boundary between fiction and non-fiction); the comics enabled participants to overcome language barriers and emboldened them to talk about sensitive issues on their own terms. Geographer Gemma Sou and John Cei Douglas (2019) created a fictional comic about the aftermath of Hurricane Maria as a way to share Sou's research findings more democratically. Although Nick Sousanis' graphic novel *Unflattening* (2015) is a theoretical work, and not the product of empirical research, it is another compelling example of how academic concepts can be expressed through a graphic medium. As Sousanis notes, comics are not simply *illustrations*; they offer a uniquely engaged and interactive means of communication, where the reader themselves 'animates' the pictures and brings the story to life (2015: 61).

What is also striking about *Lissa* is its attention to the interplay between individual stories on the one hand, and cultural forces and political circumstances on the other. This desire to spark the 'sociological imagination' – C. Wright Mills' articulation of the connection between biography and society – drives many social researchers' interest in fiction (Penfold-Mounce et al 2011; Watson 2016). And, as we explore in the following section, prose fiction can also be a productive way to do this.

Communicating with prose fiction

For social researchers interested in depicting individual characters enmeshed in complex circumstances, short stories and novels may be particularly appealing. In practical terms, prose fiction may be more accessible than comics and theatre production, which often require specialised skills, and academics who are already comfortable in writing non-fiction prose might feel willing, and able, to translate those skills to prose fiction. Moreover, as we have noted, prose fiction might capture characters' inner thoughts and feelings, and simultaneously bring their social worlds into vivid focus.

For instance, Ash Watson's sociological novel, *Into the Sea* (2020), elegantly explores this intersection of personal troubles and social issues. The novel follows Australian protagonist, Taylah, as she navigates the landscape of her mid-twenties – charting the way her relationships, career plans, personal hopes and dreams are cross-cut by broader themes of global travel, terrorism, social media and national identity. Similarly, Julia Christensen's research on homelessness in the Northwest Territories of Canada led her to write short fiction to bring to life (and give a more emotive account of) the participants' situations. In 'The Komatik Lesson', Christensen tells the story of a fictional Indigenous woman, Clara, tracing the particular path that leads Clara to become homeless, and charting moments of racism, domestic violence and Clara's fraught encounters with social services (Christensen 2009, 2012). Fictional prose can take the form, as in these examples, of novels and short stories, or even – as we discuss next – very short stories, or flash fictions (see Box 3.5).

> **Further reading: writing prose fiction**
>
> For researchers interested in writing prose fiction, good starting points include John Gardner's *The Art of Fiction* (1991) and Tim Tomlinson's (2006) overview of fiction writing, both of which discuss fiction of various lengths (from novels to short stories). Diverse perspectives on short stories can be found in the essay collection *Short Circuit* (Gebbie 2013), in which a range of writers reflect on aspects of their craft, while Sharon Oard Warner's *Writing the Novella* (2021) is a thoughtful guide to structuring novellas and offers plentiful examples of successful models to follow.

Box 3.5: 'Denial': ethnographic short stories about HIV/AIDS in South Africa

Anthropologist Tobias Hecht (also the author of an ethnographic novel and an award-wining fiction writer) created a series of very short stories based on his research about people living with HIV/AIDS in South Africa. The stories appear in a volume of creative anthropological writing (Pandian and McLean 2017) which arose from a seminar marking 30 years since the publication of Clifford and Marcus' *Writing Culture* (1986).

Hecht's stories revolve around the concept of 'denial' – this encompasses some individuals' blatant denial of facts about HIV, as well as a more ordinary denial (a kind of blinkered consciousness), which enables humans to live in the world alongside the extraordinary suffering of others. For Hecht, fiction offers a way to express such ideas, which seem to 'overflow the bounds of traditional ethnographic writing' (Hecht 2017: 133). Drawing on fieldwork as well as elements of fiction, they are what Hecht calls 'speculative anthropology ... that aims to blend what can be seen from the outside with what can be imagined about it' (2017: 133).

The stories depict a series of encounters involving an unnamed 'visitor' – whom we read as a semi-fictionalised version of Hecht himself. In one story, the visitor attends an HIV clinic, where among the resigned people receiving positive diagnoses, one smiling man seems inexplicably pleased (perhaps, the troubled visitor later reflects, the man has misunderstood and believes the diagnosis is good news because it is 'positive'). We also accompany the visitor to a shack where a woman is dying of AIDS, a story which brings into sharp focus the horror of everyday life in a city with 'two dozen toilets for half a million people, tens of thousands of whom were dying of a syndrome that causes incessant diarrhoea' (2017: 132–133).

The first story, 'Upon Arrival', deals not with HIV, but the sprawling, troubled complexity of Cape Town. In the story, the visitor arrives in the city and is greeted – shockingly – with a knife pressed into his stomach. He soon realises he is being robbed by a boy with a voice 'jagged with puberty'. The visitor fends off the boy, who then flees into the crowd. A man intervenes, apprehends the child and holds him aloft:

> The unlucky boy, airborne, raised by the scruff of the neck, flailed his limbs like an upturned beetle. A knife fell to the ground, either the knife that a moment ago was against the visitor's belly or else a different one. [The visitor] had no idea who was who, which was which, if this was the boy ... or if this was another boy with a knife and a breaking, frightened voice. The boy's green jersey was several sizes too large for his Lilliputian body. (Hecht 2017: 135)

The boy is interrogated and a crowd gathers. At the end of the story, the visitor is confronted with a choice: should he hand the boy over to the police or not? He has a chilling flash of realisation about the implications of doing so: 'the image that came to mind was that of a child in a holding cell of grown men, the sort who relish boys with breaking voices' (2017: 137). The story covers only a few pages, but is haunting and succinct, capturing a profound moment of *peripeteia* (reversal in circumstances), wherein the visitor, who initially appeared in mortal danger, now holds in his hands the fate of his attacker – a small, vulnerable boy.

Hecht's stories illustrate how researcher-authored stories might tread a subtle line between fiction and non-fiction (in fact, he suggests they might even be read as 'memoir'). Hecht is visibly present, in the reflexive persona of 'the visitor', who is both the author of – and a character within – the unfolding stories, seeking to make sense of the insensible. This blurred line is evident in other researcher-authored fictions: for instance, sociologist Toni Bruce's (2019) creative writing about sport in New Zealand occupies a space she calls 'faction', incorporating empirical research alongside autobiographical details, while Kay Inckle's (2010) fiction about self-harm draws on both formal research and her own life experiences to create a story which, like Hecht and Bruce's writing, hews close to 'creative non-fiction'.

The sense that research sometimes 'overflows the bounds' of traditional writing formats (as Hecht suggests) is a motivation for many social researchers who write fiction. Having conducted participant observation in a strip club in the southern US, anthropologist Katherine Frank wanted to convey a more complex, messy reality than could readily be communicated through formal anthropological writing: 'sex work involves moments of empowerment, intimacy, and gratification alongside moments of degradation, alienation, or disenchantment – it is this amalgamation of power and pleasure that I explore in my fiction' (2000: 483). Like the 'Denial' stories, Frank's short fiction is powerful and unsettling, raising more questions than it answers. As we noted in Chapter 2, for many social researchers, the distinctive potential for fiction is that it can tell such open-ended, unfinished stories, allowing the reader to immerse themselves in a complex world and draw their own conclusions.

Fiction, then, can allow researchers to explore and communicate the rich, ambiguous, deeply human complexity of their participants and worlds of study. Although such potential resonates clearly with the concerns of social scientists, it has also been embraced by some science, technology, engineering and mathematics (STEM) researchers. In one anthology of creative writing (including fiction) by scientists and mathematicians, Davis et al (2008) argue that while theoretical scientific research and mathematical concepts are often abstract, fiction might bring those concepts to life and also humanise the practice of scientific research (perhaps thereby building a bridge between C.P. Snow's 'two cultures'). This potential for fictional stories to illuminate the human aspects, and social consequences, of scientific ideas is the topic of our next example – the short story anthology *Infectious Futures* (see Box 3.6).

Box 3.6: *Infectious Futures*: **imagining a post-antibiotic world through science fiction**

Infectious Futures (Nesta 2015) is an anthology of short science-fiction stories about the threat of antibiotic resistance (that is, bacterial resistance to established antibiotics, exemplified by 'superbugs' such as MRSA). The six fictional stories appear alongside reflections from scientific experts.

The project was organised by Nesta, a UK innovation charity which manages the Longitude Prize – a £10 million reward given to scientific researchers who can solve a pressing global health problem. At the time, the Longitude Prize was focused on anti-microbial resistance (AMR) and was being offered for an accurate, rapid and affordable diagnostic test for bacterial infection, thus reducing and better targeting the use of antibiotics. Alongside the prize, the organisers commissioned six writers to create short fiction about the issue. They saw fiction as part of wider efforts to 'publicise, educate, and enrich the conversation around AMR' (Nesta 2015: 6). The editors observe that since humans probably evolved to tell stories 'to make sense of increasingly complex social relationships and to help us make sense of threats', the use of fiction is particularly apt, because 'today, one of the biggest threats of all is that of antimicrobial resistance' (2015: 4).

The stories explore diverse social and personal implications of antibiotic resistance (and, given that they were written before the advent of COVID-19, many are strangely prescient). In these future worlds, people seek to avoid infection at all costs, and there are depictions of political unrest, quarantines, conspiracy theories, the constant use of personal protective equipment, overworked hospital staff struggling to contain contagion, and socially isolated children who attend school remotely. 'Ayanda' (by South African writer A.S. Fields) vividly explores how something currently so easily treated as a urinary tract infection could lead to chronic pain and disability in a post-antibiotic future:

> It wasn't so much pain as a veld fire that would not go out. A never-ending slow burn. An attack. An onslaught. Like the

> mountains across the peninsula, which blackened at every change of season, Ayanda simmered in the heat. ... Life became a system of prevention. Hands were washed before going to the bathroom. Both parties showered before intimacy; to save time, this often took place in the shower. Ayanda even laid down tissue on the toilet seat in the office bathroom. It was so easy to believe that someone else's negligence was the incendiary, like an inconsiderate smoker throwing a stompie out of a car window and causing devastating mountain fires. ... Despite her efforts for a germ-free existence, Ayanda returned to the doctor's office nearly every two months when the veld fires raged anew. (Nesta 2015: 15–17)
>
> *Infectious Futures* seeks to tell stories that are not about 'an action hero in the explosive beginning or empty aftermath of a plague; but the subtler stories of living in a world where our antibiotics are failing' (2015: 7), with the hope that by bringing possible dystopian futures 'viscerally' to life, we might avoid these 'science fiction[s] becoming science fact' (2015: 5).

Infectious Futures is notable in that it was produced by commissioned authors (in contrast to fictional prose written by researchers about their own work). Similarly, the *Science into Fiction* series from UK publisher Comma Press is another instance of collaboration between scientists and fiction-writers. Here, commissioned authors produced short stories based on various areas of current research, including bio-medical advances, space travel, artificial intelligence, sleep science and climate change (Ryman 2010; Page 2012; Amos and Page 2014; Lewis and Page 2015). Scientists consulted with the writers, providing information and answering questions about their scientific research.

Both the Comma series and *Infectious Futures* collection incorporate a dialogue between scientists and writers – in both projects, scientists reflect on the likelihood of the fictional scenarios, add context about the scientific background to the stories, and sometimes point out the shortcomings of particular stories as a means to share or represent research (see also Chapter 4). Such dialogues allow readers to evaluate the stories, but also perhaps open up the possibility that fiction might in turn inform or influence researchers (for example, Bassett et al 2013).

Such researcher–writer collaborations (and the potential for mutual influence) are not unique to STEM fields. Novelist Margaret Elphinstone worked closely with archaeologist Caroline Wickham-Jones when writing a novel set in Mesolithic Scotland. Wickham-Jones' input allowed Elphinstone's novel to achieve a scholarly rigour, and the novel was subsequently reviewed by academics and used in university teaching alongside conventional research outputs (Elphinstone and Wickham-Jones 2012: 535). At the same time, Elphinstone's writerly questions about the details of everyday life in the Mesolithic led Wickham-Jones to interrogate her own research in new ways: 'I started to consider aspects of prehistoric life that had not occurred to me before: "So what *did* they have for breakfast?"' (Elphinstone and Wickham-Jones 2012: 536).

As *Infectious Futures* also powerfully illustrates, fiction has a unique power to bring to life possible worlds and imagined futures which have not occurred. It is this potential which informs our final case study, S.R. Toliver's *Endarkened Storywork* (2021) (see Box 3.7).

Box 3.7: *Endarkened Storywork*: **speculative fiction and social justice**

Endarkened Storywork is a speculative fiction novel, written by US sociologist S.R. Toliver as a means of sharing her research (although Toliver's work goes beyond fiction as 'dissemination').

Set in 2085, Toliver's novel transports us into a dystopian world divided into 'Endarkened' (or Black) people, and a ruling class of 'Dreamers' who have perfected a scientific procedure by which they can extract Endarkened people's dreams. As the protagonist, Jane (an Endarkened woman), explains:

> The bluer the eyes, the more successful the programming. That's what they tell us anyway. The Dreamers' eyes are brown, amber,

green, grey, or hazel. My eyes and the eyes of all the Endarkened are different shades of blue, some as piercing as the color of LED lights and others as bright as the sky on a sunny day. I sometimes wonder if the brightness of our eyes is what stops us from dreaming. Darkness is the space of dreams; it's the place where imagination can grow; it serves as a backdrop for the magical … to dream is to imagine something better, to envision a reality that's different from this one. (Toliver 2021: 1)

Jane works for the Dreamers' regime, but she soon discovers and joins an underground resistance of Endarkened people. Among them, she encounters a group of young women engaged in writing speculative, fictional stories – and Jane realises that through such acts of creativity and imagination, the ability to dream can be restored. (An arc which recalls the hero's journey, as Jane returns home with an 'elixir', transformed by her quest.)

The novel emerged from Toliver's own qualitative research with Black girls in the US, which entailed workshops where participants wrote speculative fiction. (Notably, the girls' stories in turn incorporated references and homages to many *other* fictions, such as popular television series, films, books, manga and anime.) The young resistance women whom Jane encounters in the novel are lightly fictionalised versions of the real research participants, and the participants' short stories appear in full within the novel.

Toliver's approach to fiction and storytelling is grounded in multiple influences. She situates her work in contrast to 'enlightenment' traditions, which privilege objectivity, rationality and truth, and argues instead for the power of 'endarkened' stories, which celebrate Black ways of knowing, telling and sharing (2021: xvi). She reflects on the role of storytelling in Black and Indigenous societies, noting the role of griots, 'who were the scholars of the African nations' (2021: xv). Toliver also invokes the African folk character Anansi – trickster and god of stories – who epitomises the role of storytelling in Black culture and history, where oppression might be resisted through cunning and wit. Another key influence is the literature of Afrofuturism – science fiction and fantasy by Black writers (such as Octavia Butler) – which, Toliver argues, is a means by which Black authors might 'reclaim and recover the past, counter negative and elevate positive realities that exist in the present, and create new possibilities for the future' (2021: xxi). Toliver's 'Black feminist epistemology' also draws on feminist thinkers who have called for scholarship which is spiritual, creative, emotional, and focused on community and social justice (2021: xvii), and where stories are recognised as a legitimate form of knowledge (see also Hurston 1996; Hill Collins 2014; Nadar 2014).

Toliver's work is an excellent example of the multiple possibilities for fiction in research – her study is inspired by existing Afrofuturist fiction, the participants wrote their own fictions, *and* Toliver communicates her findings via a piece of researcher-authored fiction. Here, fictional stories are simultaneously a research method, a means of sharing research, a core feature of everyday life, a form of resistance, as well as a tool for envisioning new possibilities and changing the world.

Concluding thoughts

In this chapter, we have highlighted a wide range of approaches to fiction. These illustrative examples show how using 'fiction' in research might mean constructing intricately imagined fantasy worlds, telling semi-autobiographical stories, performing verbatim pieces composed of real interview transcripts, or even answering the simple question 'what happens next?'

We have discussed research which engages with existing works of fiction, research which invites participants to create fictions, and research which uses fiction to share research insights. Throughout, we have pointed to the unstable nature of boundaries between these concepts, showing how such categories frequently blur and overlap.

These cases show the rich and varied potential for employing fiction in research. However, readers may already be thinking about the challenges that might be involved in using fiction in some of these ways or the difficulties and dilemmas that may be provoked in selecting the 'right' approach for any particular piece of research. In the next chapter, we look more closely at the difficulties, complexities, ethical issues and considerations that researchers should bear in mind if using fiction.

Reflective questions

- How do you plan to employ fiction? Will you use fiction to 'think with'? To conduct research through participant-created stories? To share research findings? In more than one of these ways? (Or none of these – our list may not be exhaustive!)
- Are you interested in the process of creating fiction, in the fictional product, or both?
- Consider the different rationales for combining fiction and research (Chapter 2). Do you think some fictional media (for example, prose, drama, or comics) might be better suited to different objectives?

Reflective exercises

1. Compelling fictional stories often hinge on scenarios in which a character (or characters) faces new or challenging circumstances. Story completion scholars Braun et al refer to these as 'cliff-hanger' situations, and their work shows how even seemingly mundane moments of change (for example, 'a man has decided to remove his body hair') provide very effective story openings. The other case studies similarly introduce us to characters confronting difficult and/or pivotal moments: for example, a vulnerable young person's carefully planned journey goes awry. In the other stories, a young woman is at risk of developing breast cancer. A man needs a kidney transplant. A couple take a dying relative to hospital. A woman is suffering from a painful infection in a world without antibiotic treatments. A stranger arrives in a city fraught with violence and danger. A woman is trapped in a dystopian regime which exercises control over people's minds. Such scenarios draw us in, inviting us to discover how these circumstances arose, how the characters will respond, and what will happen next.

Try to capture this narrative energy by identifying a tense moment or cliff-hanger situation relevant to your own research. Write freely for 20 minutes about how a character experiences and responds to those circumstances. You could create a composite or imagined character, or you might follow the example of Tobias Hecht and S.R. Toliver and create a third-person character who is a fictionalised version of yourself – the researcher – embarking on a new or difficult project. This exercise may or may not lead to a polished piece of fiction, but exploring such ideas can help to identify and harness fictional potentials in your work.

2. Reflecting on other researchers' use of fiction can help to refine and clarify your own approach to research-fiction. Read in more depth about one or two pieces of research-fiction (you might draw them from this chapter or find other examples). Consider what the researchers aimed to achieve through fiction. Do you think they achieved their aims? Do you find their use of fiction effective? What seemed to work and what did not? Are there insights or techniques you could apply to your own work? What would you do differently?

4

Difficult questions

This chapter:

- Raises some key challenges which researchers using fiction may face.
- Highlights that fiction may not be the right choice for all research projects.
- Explores if and how research-fiction can be evaluated (as research, as fiction, or as something else).
- Discusses the implications of decisions around how to present, frame and publish research-fictions.
- Explores some of the ethical issues raised by combining research and fiction.

Introduction

Many writings about research and fiction read as something of a manifesto. However, as we explore in this chapter, it is also important that researchers ask difficult questions about this approach, including the ethical and practical issues it raises (Gibson 2021).

We draw inspiration here from the 'difficult questions' that Jennifer Mason advises qualitative researchers ask themselves (2002: 4–5). Like Mason, we do not offer prescriptive ethical guidelines or 'correct' answers to these conundrums; instead we invite researchers to interrogate their own assumptions and critically explore how fiction could function in their own work.

The particular difficult questions researchers and fiction-writers face will be specific to their project and aims, but in this chapter we explore five broad questions we think are particularly relevant to many researchers using fiction:

1. Is fiction right for my research?
2. How can we evaluate research-fictions?
3. Is research-fiction good fiction, and does it matter?
4. How should research-fiction be presented?
5. What new ethical issues does research-fiction raise?

Is fiction right for my research?

Perhaps the most important question which researchers must ask themselves is whether the use of fiction is the right choice for their research. Readers of this book are likely interested in, perhaps even excited by, the potential of research-fiction. However, it is important to consider whether such an approach is compatible with their particular research aims, questions and the context in which they are working. We would suggest that fiction is not necessarily 'good' for all projects, purposes or audiences. It also need not be used in isolation. Depending on a researcher's aims and objectives, they may wish to combine fictional approaches with data collection, analysis and dissemination via traditional 'non-fiction' methods, which may include academic articles but also blogs, animations, policy briefings, media articles or documentary films. In fact, some prominent advocates of innovative writing, Donna Haraway (1991) and Laurel Richardson (1993), explicitly state that they do not wish to do away with 'traditional' academic prose, but rather open up the academy to experimental and *multiple* ways of using language and sharing knowledge, which can bring about a recognition of the partiality of all forms.

Where fiction plays a role in data generation, researchers will need to ask questions about the status of that fiction and whether it constitutes or prompts useful and relevant data in relation to the questions they have set out to answer. This might involve consideration of, for example, how exactly participant-produced fiction relates to participants' lived experiences (for example, Phillips and Kara 2021: 75). Do such texts reveal salient or meaningful issues in their lives (for example, North 2017)? Or do their stories express what they *wish* could happen in reality (Satchwell et al 2018: 15)? Do fictions reveal people's shared cultural knowledge and discourses (Clarke et al 2019)? Additionally, if fiction plays a role in data *analysis*, researchers will need to articulate how exactly fiction is 'good' for this purpose; for instance, does writing fiction enable a researcher to come to new appreciations of their data (Richardson and St. Pierre 2005; Phillips and Kara 2021: 175–176)? And if the fiction is analysed, does it constitute a form of qualitative data, or should it be approached as an 'imaginative literary text' (McNicol 2019: 242)?

Researchers should also consider the longer-term aims of their research. Is the goal to influence policy or practices in a particular area? Perhaps it is to change people's minds or behaviour on a particular matter? Or is the research primarily envisaged as a contribution to knowledge in their discipline or field? Researchers should consider the audiences they will need to speak to in order for their research to have the impact they seek. Research-fiction is likely to be interpreted as more or less legitimate knowledge in different contexts. However, it is important not to draw these lines too heavily; even in contexts where 'hard facts' are valued, there may still be a place for stories to engage audiences such that the 'facts' will be heard and acted upon.

Similarly, researchers in different disciplines may find varying levels of comfort with the use of fiction in research. As Leavy (2012, 2013, 2022) and Watson (2016) variously highlight, there are particular affinities between sociology, qualitative methods, critical theory and fiction. In disciplinary or sub-disciplinary contexts where the method is seen as novel, and perhaps particularly when used by more junior or otherwise marginalised researchers (see Dumitrica 2010), researchers may find the rigour of their research liable to challenge or face the risk that interest in their 'creative' methods overshadows interest in the knowledge it produces. Furthermore, if a primary aim is to contribute to knowledge in a particular field or discipline, it is also important to consider how a piece of research-fiction might be referenced, critiqued and cited by others working in the same field.

How can we evaluate research-fiction?

Assuming that research-fiction fits with the aims and objectives of the researcher, we might also ask whether the research-fiction produced is of good quality. There is widespread agreement that 'standard' criteria for evaluating research (for example, rigour, reliability, significance) require, at a minimum, some modification in order to be useful in relation to research-fictions, or arts-based methods more generally. Various approaches have been suggested.

One proposal is to assess the value of a research-fiction by considering its impact in the world. Leavy asks us to consider the 'substantive contribution' of research fictions: what does the work 'contribute to our understanding' of a topic (2022: 203)? Does it 'disturb and disrupt' familiar ideas and make audiences reassess their assumptions (Barone and Eisner 2012: 101)? Does a creative output 'have an appreciable effect on the audience's understanding of, or appreciation for, the study findings' (Lafrenière and Cox 2013: 322)? To this end, researchers may systematically solicit feedback from participants and/or audiences: for example, Lewando Hundt et al (2019) asked over 1,000 audience members at their research-based play to reflect on how the performance impacted them, and Christensen (2012) asked for feedback from First Nations community members on her story about a fictional Indigenous woman. Researchers might want to ask, for instance, whether people depicted in a fiction recognise their experiences (if a story 'rings true'), and how/whether the fiction has changed an audience's views or sparked new insights.

Such approaches suggest that the value of fiction emerges through interaction with audiences. However, as Watson (2011) notes, not all audiences will necessarily be sympathetic and the success of research-fiction depends, in part, on the receptiveness of audiences to this approach. And, of course, all requests for feedback will depend on readers'/audiences' readiness to respond (for example, although Lewando Hundt et al received positive and detailed feedback, only around 30 per cent of the theatre attendees completed the questionnaire [Lewando Hundt et al

2019]). Researchers who publish prose fiction might find it more difficult to solicit feedback than researchers who use live performance (although digitising research-fiction could help to address this issue).

Alongside audience/reader response, some social research scholars have developed systematic criteria for assessing artistic and fictional works. Fictional outputs might be assessed with reference to: their role as public scholarship, their degree of trustworthiness, resonance, aesthetics, creativity, thoughtfulness, verisimilitude, empathetic engagement, use of personal style, as well as adherence to ethical research standards (Leavy 2022: 197–205, see also 2013: 77–91); their contribution to knowledge, credibility (or a 'real-seeming' account), aesthetic merit, demonstration of researcher reflexivity, and the affective impact on a reader (Richardson and St. Pierre 2005); or the demonstration of technical/artistic mastery, and whether the work accurately represents some aspect of the data and reflects rigorous data collection (Lafrenière and Cox 2013).

Such evaluation criteria may be particularly useful for qualitative researchers. In fact, although Patricia Leavy notes that research-based fiction is not the *same* as research (for example, 2022: 198), she suggests the standards for evaluating qualitative research can be 'transformed' and productively applied to fiction (Leavy 2013: 79). For instance, whereas qualitative research often aims for truth and fidelity to data, research-based fiction might seek *truthfulness* and plausibility. Most criteria also accommodate an attention to the 'artistry' of a fictional output – for example, Leavy argues for consideration of the author's use of 'literary tools', with attention to such issues as language, description, detail, metaphor, symbolism, plotting, voice, characterisation, and the piece's narrative coherence (Leavy 2022: 201–203). We discuss these aesthetic considerations further in the following section.

However, while there is widespread agreement that the usual methods for judging the quality of research and outputs may fall short in relation to research-fictions or arts-based methods, not all agree on the need for alternative standards (see Lafrenière and Cox 2013). Bochner, for example, is critical of the quest for 'criteria' against which 'alternative' ethnographies might be judged. He relates such 'incessant' searches to 'insecurities about [social scientists'] scientific stature' (Bochner 2000: 267), though arguably this critique could apply to other disciplines. Bochner highlights that there are no culture or value-free standards against which research and writing can be judged and attempts to devise such criteria risk stifling the creative potential and impact which 'alternative' research methods offer. He asks: 'I wonder, what is it we are not talking about when we are talking about criteria? Instead of asking, how can this be true? we could ask, what if this were true? What then?' (2000: 267). Researchers who use fiction will need to decide which methods of evaluation or criteria (if any) are applicable to their work and standards for research in their own discipline.

Is research-fiction good fiction, and does it matter?

As we have noted, when evaluating research-fictions (whether through formal criteria or more informally) readers and audiences will often compare the work against wider artistic and aesthetic expectations of the genre.

However, such criteria might not be applicable to all research-fictions. For instance, Phillips and Kara embrace the 'strategic scruffiness' of 'queer' writing: although polished (fictional) products are *one* possible outcome of creative writing in the research process, they argue that insights can also be gained from 'bad' writing and unfinished stories (2021: 177–179). For others, conventional standards of 'artistry' are less important than whether a piece resonates with a target audience or with participant-authors (Satchwell et al 2020: 878), and some researchers are emphatic that their fiction should be evaluated *only* as a contribution to research and not as literature (Park-Kang 2015: 374). From these perspectives, measuring the quality of fiction (by conventional standards) is not necessarily a primary concern. But, depending on their aims and research goals, researchers may find it appropriate and relevant to ask how research-based fiction measures up against other works of fiction, and whether it could be considered 'good' in those terms.

The question of whether academic researchers have the ability to produce 'good' fiction is somewhat debated. It may be that researchers, particularly those who are already confident writers, are able to turn those skills to fiction-writing (for example, Banks and Banks 1998: 18). However, Gibson (2021) notes that doctoral training does not usually equip academics with the skills to write non-academic or fictional texts, and Lafrenière and Cox (2013: 330) exhort researchers using artistic methods to work alongside a trained practitioner until they develop proficiency in the craft themselves. Similarly, Anderson (2007) warns that some advocates of ethnodrama have underestimated the importance of stage craft and skill in performance storytelling and thus encourages researchers to work with and learn from experienced theatre practitioners. Where the 'quality' of fiction is important, researchers will need to assess their own ability to produce work of the necessary standard.

Regardless of the skills of the writer, there are some particular difficulties which the creators of research-fictions may face in creating 'good' fiction: the risk of didacticism, and the potential challenges of telling a 'good story'. These challenges relate to possible tensions between the aims of research and fiction.

Is the work didactic? (And does it matter?)

A distinctive issue for researchers communicating with fiction is the possibility that their work – in seeking to educate and inform, or to convey a particular point of view – may be considered didactic. Of course, some forms of fiction place great emphasis on instructing listeners and readers, or teaching moral 'lessons'; examples include pre-20th-century literature, fables, fairy tales, oral folktales, and many Chinese and African fictional traditions (for example, Casement 1987; Bettelheim 1989; Salesses 2021; Osei-Tutu 2023). However, for many readers and writers of contemporary Western literary fiction, 'didactic' carries negative associations, suggesting a work is heavy-handed, patronising or artless (for example, Repp 2012; Self 2014).

Writers whose work spans research and fiction are often alert to this risk (Saldaña 2005: 14; Case, in Barone and Eisner 2012: 117; Crockett Thomas 2022: 10; Watson 2022). Although Iris Murdoch was both a scholar and novelist, she firmly rejected the possibility of using fiction to promote academic ideas or political agendas, noting that 'as soon as a writer says to himself, "I must try to change society in such and such ways by my writing," he is likely to damage his work' (1999: 17).

Whether this presents a problem will depend on a researcher's perspective, aims, their intended audience and the audience's expectations (as we have noted, some research-based fiction is not intended to be measured against conventional literary standards). However, writers who do wish to avoid the charge of didacticism may want to reflect on this difficult question. Of course, strategies exist to address this issue (and many of the pointers we discuss in Chapter 5 offer writers ways to 'show' rather than 'tell' ideas), but one approach can be to focus on creating complex, rounded characters through whom to tell a story (for example, Murdoch 1999: 120–121; Lafrenière and Cox 2013: 330). Additionally, while Robert McKee observes that fiction which aims to convince readers of a particular position risks becoming a 'thinly disguised sermon' (1997: 120–121), he also notes that writers can mitigate this through sustained engagement with *other*, contradictory positions, enabling them to tell a more nuanced and subtle story.

Are good research and good fiction compatible?

Although there are no universal criteria for what constitutes 'good' fiction, certain tenets of compelling storytelling are widely endorsed, for instance, the idea that effective stories will expose a character's flaws and weaknesses and 'force the protagonist to question their deepest beliefs' (Storr 2020: 90). Or that in fiction, 'we stretch towards the bests and the worsts because story – when it is art – is not about the middle ground of human experience' (McKee 1997: 207; see also Nussbaum 2007: 90).

Stories which embrace these principles are likely to be dramatic and engaging, but for some researchers these tenets may present challenges. For example, is it always desirable, ethical or practical for a social researcher to focus on participants' flaws and weaknesses, or depict their confrontation with the 'worsts' of human experience? Do the stories which emerge from the research (or which participants/researchers want to tell) fit readily into the mould of a 'good' story?

In the anthology *Infectious Futures*, such conflicts arose when some fiction writers wanted to tell disturbing and apocalyptic stories about the future of anti-microbial resistance. Such high-stakes situations make for compelling fiction. However, scientists engaged in the project were concerned that stories which primarily generate fear 'can lead to denial and paralysis rather than positive behaviour change' and might 'help, rather than hinder, in bringing about the dystopian future they depict so vividly' (Nesta 2015: 10).

Similar tensions can emerge in participant-authored stories. In story-completion exercises, respondents sometimes create outlandish tales (incorporating, for example, vampires or sudden death), rather than reproducing more ordinary discourses (Braun et al 2019: 139). Such participants might well be seeking to tell a story which is 'good' by conventional standards – one which is entertaining, amusing or surprising. In collaboratively created fiction, participants are also sometimes drawn to tell dramatic stories (of murder or incest, for instance), rather than fictions which reflect their everyday experiences (Raynor 2016: 111). And in some cases, researchers or participants may need to balance the pull of a gripping storyline or fascinating characters against questions about the story's impact. For example, negative representations of members of a community may be received poorly by an audience drawn from that community (Phillips et al 2020: 42–43), and although casting certain characters as villains or antagonists can create an engaging fictional narrative, it could also harm real people on whom those characters are based (Satchwell et al 2018: 28). Where a researcher has such concerns, they may choose to intervene or redirect participants' stories, although this can raise new difficult questions if the fictions are intended to reflect participants' own voices.

Research-based fictions also exist within a wider context of popular fictions. If an issue or group is commonly portrayed in a particular manner, researchers and participants might wish to tell a *different* kind of story – perhaps emphasising resilience instead of victimhood, or focusing on ordinary experiences rather than sensational incidents. In a similar vein, Leavy notes that researchers should be alert to common stereotypical depictions of participants and actively seek to counteract them (Leavy 2022: 205). Researchers may thus need to engage with the question of what sorts of stories audiences might *expect* to hear, and perhaps ask whether some popular, common or successful fictions are not necessarily 'good' stories in the context of the research.

Of course, as we have noted, the extent to which researchers will be concerned with these risks and challenges will depend on their particular aims and intentions for their work, and how they intend it to be read and interpreted – which leads us to our next difficult question.

How should research-fiction be presented?
How is research-based fiction framed and explained?

Many of the 'difficult' questions we have raised so far underline the significance of how researchers frame and present their fictions. In contemplating these questions, researchers will need to reflect on the status they claim for any research-based fiction: how do they intend it to be read and interpreted by their audience? The status claims made may be both explicit and implicit in the ways that fiction is introduced and presented to potential readers and audiences.

One important decision is how a researcher names the work they have produced. Many terms exist for fiction which emerges from (or plays a role in) research. Patricia Leavy (2013) writes of 'fiction-based research', wherein social researchers reimagine their practice through creating fictional works, and she devised the term 'social fiction' for fiction 'written by researchers in any field [which] reflects their social research concerns or expertise' (Leavy 2022: 3). Fictionalised work inspired by research might variously be called 'creative non-fiction', 'faction', 'ethnographic fiction' or 'memoir' (for example, Schmidt 1984; Inckle 2010; Pandian and McLean 2017; Bruce 2019). Lewando Hundt et al refer to their work as 'research-based theatre' (2019: 1). Satchwell et al present their work as neither research nor fiction but as 'story' (2020: 887), while Christensen similarly describes her fiction as 'research storytelling' (Christensen 2009: 238). And Elphinstone and Wickham-Jones explore how the 'informed novel' can arise through sustained academic engagement (2012: 532). The choice of terminology can suggest whether a piece is conceived primarily as a *type of research* or as a *type of fiction*, although it often highlights the ambiguous nature of such work, which can seem to occupy a space *in-between* research and fiction. Researchers may want to consider what terms they use to describe their own fiction, and what this implies about how it should be appraised (as fiction, as research, as both, or as something else entirely).

Another important consideration in framing research-fiction is how a researcher chooses to present and introduce their work. This includes decisions about layout, formatting and any illustrations which can (as with naming) act to position a piece as more or less academic, literary or artistic. For instance, fictions which include visual elements, such as illustrations – or fiction told primarily through images – can be one way to indicate that a piece differs from traditional academic texts and is intended for non-academic audiences (for example, Sousanis 2015; Hamdy and Nye 2017; Sou and Cei Douglas 2019).

Presenting research-fiction also entails decisions about how (and whether) to provide a written introduction or explanation. As Cate Watson notes, when fiction is used to share research findings, it is often 'swaddled within a researchly paratext' (2011: 403) which outlines the context of the research and data, and signals to the reader how the fiction is intended to be read. Although Watson's reference to 'swaddling' implies an ambivalence towards these explanations, Barone and Eisner liken such paratexts to the preamble that sometimes precedes a concert or play, which allows the audience to more fully appreciate a work of art (2012: 59–61).

Paratexts can take various forms. In performances, they may be presented in a printed programme or as a verbal introduction. With regard to published fiction, many options exist. *The Sociological Review*, for instance, publishes sociological fiction followed by an exegesis which 'unpacks and contextualises' the story. S.R. Toliver's *Endarkened Storywork* (2021) contains a novel which can be read as a standalone work, but also includes several optional 'reading companion' chapters describing Toliver's qualitative research and the theoretical background to her work. In contrast, Ash Watson's sociological-fiction novel, *Into the Sea* (2020), contains a very brief introduction. Patricia Leavy likewise favours minimal explanations in her social fictions, preferring that each novel 'stand … on its own as an artistic work' (Leavy

2013: 74), although some of her works include questions at the end, to prompt individual reflection or guide group/student discussion (for example, Leavy 2019). And, although a piece may be presented with little explanation in one venue, researchers can of course publish explanatory or academic pieces elsewhere (as both Patricia Leavy and Ash Watson have done). Fiction might also be presented alongside paratexts *and* original research data, allowing a reader to directly compare the fiction and the data which inspired it (Wolf 1992; Breen 2017).

Decisions about whether to include a paratext, its content and its position in the text (that is, as preface, exegesis, footnotes, endnotes or a distinct commentary article) should be consistent with researchers' aims and objectives for a given project or output. This will also be influenced by the intended audience and their expectations. For example, if authors anticipate a level of scepticism about the status of research-fiction as 'real' research, they may include an exegesis with emphasises the rigour of methods of data collection and analysis. They may also choose to discuss exactly which elements of a fiction are drawn from data and which are invented (Frank 2000: 485; Rabbiosi and Vanolo 2017: 272). However, researchers whose primary aim in writing fiction is to disrupt notions of academic/scientific authority may reject the need for a paratext altogether or may choose to write one in such a way that the distinction between commentary and fiction is blurred, or they may choose to position a paratext at the end to centre the fictional work. Finally, while paratexts or data excerpts can allow readers to better interpret and evaluate a work of fiction, they can risk reinscribing the work as a piece of scholarly research rather than a creative work, which again raises the question of whether the work will be experienced by readers in the same way as conventional fiction (for example, Bruce 2019: 67).

How will fictional outputs be shared?

Not all research-fictions will be shared beyond the researcher-participant team. For instance, where fiction is a tool for data collection or analysis, publication may not be appropriate to the research aims. However, in many cases, research-based fictional outputs will be shared with an external audience, through publication and/or performance.

When research-based prose fiction is published, researchers will need to find a publisher or publication venue. This might be a literary publisher – for instance, the Comma Press short story collections discussed in Chapter 3, which paired scientific researchers with fiction-writers, were published by a literary press (and promoted primarily *as* 'works of fiction' rather than 'research collaborations'). However, this approach is relatively unusual, and more frequently, as Gibson (2021) notes, research-based fictional outputs are published by academic presses or in scholarly journals. To some extent, this is a product of academic culture. Academics at all career stages may feel pressure to publish in traditional outlets and journals, but students, early career researchers, academics on precarious contracts, or otherwise marginalised scholars may find that non-traditional and creative work is a particularly risky proposition (Hill Collins 2014; Gibson 2021; Phillips and Kara 2021: 174).

An exception to Gibson's observation (that research-fictions are most often published in academic fora) is research-based drama. While these may be published as written scripts, typically such works are also performed and/or filmed, and made available, sometimes via video sharing platforms, to broader audiences. Nevertheless, researchers' decisions regarding the performance venue (for example, a university, commercial or community theatre), casting (which might include participants, researchers or professional actors), cost of entry and marketing may still align these works with 'traditional' academic outputs, activism or artistic endeavours (see Taylor et al 2017).

Academic publications can bring fiction to the attention of other academics, including those in other disciplines, allowing knowledge and insights to be shared and built upon. They can also provide a valuable pedagogical resource – some research-fictions specifically aim to foster discussion among students (Douglas and Carless 2009; Watson 2020). However, like the use of scholarly paratexts, publication in academic venues risks framing a work as primarily 'academic', thereby counteracting the broad 'accessibility' that fiction is thought to bring in the first place.[1] General readers are unlikely to discover, or seek out, research-based fiction in academic journals. And, importantly, when academic journals are paywalled, non-institutional readers may be unable to access them at all (see also Gibson 2021). Ash Watson (2016) writes compellingly of the potential of sociologically informed novels to realise Michael Burawoy's vision of a 'public sociology' (Watson 2016: 434). However, the practicalities of *reaching* those 'publics' can be a complex matter. Who exactly is the 'public', and how will they encounter research-based fiction?

The research literature frequently characterises fiction as 'engaging' and 'accessible'. Although there are strong arguments for this point of view, another difficult question for researchers is whether fiction *is* automatically more engaging than other outputs (Barone and Eisner 2012: 69; Pandian and McLean 2017: 23; Gibson 2021). Fiction can be poorly written or boring, while academic work can be compelling and eloquent. Additionally, popular *non*-fiction documentaries and books (which may incorporate significant research) can be equally as impactful and well-received as popular fiction. Fictional prose might also be less widely and enthusiastically consumed than is often supposed; indicatively, only around 40 per cent of US adults reported reading *any* novels or short stories during 2017, and book sales are often dominated by a very small number of best-sellers (for example, Flood 2018). And, as Margery Wolf warns, there is a particular risk that experimental or post-modern works of research-based fiction might alienate readers, perhaps becoming comprehensible only to 'a small elite made up primarily of first-world academics with literary inclinations' (Wolf 1992: 138). In short, not all fictional outputs are necessarily accessible to all people.

For researchers inspired by the potential of fiction, such questions may feel uncomfortable or disheartening, but we think they are not insurmountable – critical engagement with these questions can allow researchers to create more robust fictions and forestall scepticism from potential audiences. With regard to audience engagement, researchers who use fiction may choose to incorporate ongoing or iterative feedback throughout the creative process, testing and refining a work (for example, Lewando Hundt et al 2019). Additionally, researchers can pay close attention to the kinds of fiction which resonate with particular audiences/ participants, for instance through working in Indigenous storytelling traditions (Christensen 2012), or engaging with young people's interest in popular fictions including TV series or films (Toliver 2021; Davies 2023).

What new ethical issues does research-fiction raise?

One powerful justification for the use of fiction is the potential to create more ethical representations of research data. However, ethical decisions are complex, and in some cases, fiction might not achieve these aims, and might even create new ethical problems.

Is fictionalisation always desirable?

Ethical concerns often drive researchers to fictionalise participants' identities and words. However, in some circumstances, preserving real identities can be more appropriate. For instance, in the graphic novel *Lissa*, Anna, Layla and their families are 'composite characters' and the storyline is fictional. However, Hamdy and Nye also chose *not* to fictionalise other aspects of their research: some doctors who actually treated injured protestors in the Egyptian revolution are depicted in *Lissa* with their real names. Additionally, *Lissa*'s graphics include actual protest graffiti made during the revolution. The decision to name and credit doctors and graffiti artists was an ethical one, intended to honour those individuals' bravery; as Coleman Nye notes, co-opting real people's actions or art for the authors' fiction could be construed as a form of exploitative 'Western academic tourism' (Hamdy and Nye 2017: 273), something they wished to avoid.

Relatedly, since the later 20th century, the explicit motivation for much qualitative social research has been to give 'voice' to participants, particularly people marginalised in society or overlooked by academic research (such as children and disabled people), and individuals may participate in research specifically because they want their voices to be heard (for example, Douedari et al 2021; Sudarsan et al 2022; but see Mazzei and Jackson 2012; Facca et al 2020 for post-structuralist/post-modern critiques).

However, where *fictional* representations are used in place of empirical data, participants risk becoming 'absent voices in their own stories' (Gibson 2021: 660).

Participants themselves might thus feel that their real words and experiences are obscured or supplanted by fictions, but there are also potential risks if *readers* perceive a distance between the fiction and empirical data. For example, some audiences (including journalists) might see fiction as abstract or irrelevant, preferring clearly factual stories about real individuals (Parr 2021). As Will Gibson notes, research-based fiction risks appearing more 'like a parable than an *example* or *evidence*' since it lacks the credibility of data which alerts people to a '*real* social problem' (2021: 660, emphasis in original). Additionally, in contexts where participants' voices are already viewed as unreliable or lacking in authority (as might be the case with children, for instance), representing participants' perspectives through fiction could even reinforce such perceptions. The possibility exists, then, that contrary to researchers' aims, fictionalised work could be *less* effective at empowering participants or inciting change than non-fictional accounts.

Might fiction cause harm to research participants?

Many researchers turn to fiction because of its potential to represent participants in an ethical manner. Patricia Leavy emphasises the potential for fiction, when written compassionately and sensitively and without recourse to stereotypes, to promote understanding about other people's lives (2022: 55). And Kay Inckle argues that fiction can be a way to tell complex and nuanced human stories, thereby avoiding the representational 'violence' of objectifying accounts which, for instance, might reduce people to medical diagnoses (2010: 29).

However, fiction does not guarantee that such 'representational violence' will be avoided. For instance, harm might occur if a research participant recognises aspects of their account or experience in a published research-fiction but finds the overall story out-of-step with, or worse, insensitive to, their own. We cannot assume that this would necessarily *feel* any less harmful to said participant in a fictional work than in a research report.

In conventional research, there is the potential for outputs to be assessed by participants or interviewees who can speak to its validity; does it represent their lives? In contrast, participants might find it difficult to dispute representations of their lives which appear as fictional outputs, since the fictional format allows for gaps to be filled and details to be added or changed, and since fictions, by definition, do not make the same truth claims as empirically based research texts.

Where fiction draws heavily on the account of a particular participant, the risk of harm again arises if that individual might become identifiable. Researchers can address such issues by discussing this possibility with participants (see, for example, Crockett Thomas et al 2021). And, as we have noted, many researchers using fiction do seek to address these issues by eliciting feedback from participants at *all stages* of the process, or by working with participants collaboratively, to ensure that participants have input or a 'right to reply' to the fictional stories as they are created.

Additionally, where participant-produced or collaborative fictions explore sensitive, intimate or emotional issues which participants might find distressing, researchers should also be mindful of the potential for harm at the stage of fictional production. This is arguably a particular concern in drama which involves research participants re-enacting painful experiences (see, for example, Boal 1995; Raynor 2019; Conrad 2023). Conrad (2023), who produced applied theatre with 'street-involved youth' in Canada, reflects on the risks of 're-traumatising' participants and discusses how she and her team used strategies to reduce stress and support their vulnerable and marginalised participants.

In some cases, where the use of fiction is written into the research from the outset, consent and involvement can be clearly agreed upon with participants. However, in some instances, consent and feedback might be more difficult to obtain. For example, Leavy's fiction draws on multiple research studies, and she also specifically acknowledges the contribution of everyday experiences and liminal encounters (Leavy 2022: 69; 88; see also Inckle 2010; Farrant 2014; Rabbiosi and Vanolo 2017: 6). In such cases, or where plans to create research-fictions arise during or (perhaps many years) after a period of data collection, not everyone concerned can be consulted. This need not *necessarily* rule out the inclusion of such data and, indeed, it would be impossible to exclude the influence of cumulative knowledge in analysis and writing. However, this does raise the possibility that some contributors/participants could feel misled about the nature of their interactions with researchers, and arguably heightens possibilities for the representational violence discussed earlier, particularly if individuals see themselves as (mis)represented in published works.

A further risk is that *readers or audiences* might 'misinterpret' fiction. For instance, although fiction offers a powerful means to evoke empathy for characters (for example, Leavy 2022: 12–13), conjuring empathy through fiction is a complex process open to pitfalls – characters who are intended to be empathetic might be disliked by readers, or readers might feel empathy towards the 'wrong' characters (Keen 2006). Fiction intended to be ambiguous, open-ended or polyvocal is of course especially likely to be interpreted in multiple, perhaps unpredictable ways; researchers may want to reflect on what it means to relinquish control of their work and throw it open to readers' interpretations, even if these interpretations run counter to their authorial intentions.

A final ethical issue to consider is that of attribution and authorship. Where a piece of fiction is collaborative, or jointly created, questions may arise about *whose* work it is. For example, in the play *Passing On*, playwright Mike Kenny is credited as the author of the play and holds the copyright – a decision achieved after discussion with participants (Lewando Hundt et al 2019). However, where a piece of fiction draws heavily on participants' words or experiences (or in the case of verbatim theatre, is comprised *solely* of their words), such decisions are not straightforward, and researchers may want to reflect on and negotiate with participants how best to attribute authorship of a fictional piece.

Concluding thoughts

We suggest that these questions reflect, and contribute to, the rapidly evolving field of research-fiction. Thanks to the pioneering work of many researchers, 'fiction as method' (to borrow Patricia Leavy's phrase) now has a level of credibility (particularly in the humanities and social sciences) such that it is possible, and necessary, to move beyond enthusiastic 'manifestos' for research-fiction and also engage with some of the more difficult questions it raises (see also Gibson 2021). As researchers continue to engage with the possibilities presented by fiction, they may encounter and articulate new difficult questions.

The questions we have outlined here are not exhaustive, but we hope they will prompt further discussion about some of the problems, pitfalls and challenges of combining research and fiction, enabling researchers to anticipate obstacles and refine their research planning and practice. These questions are 'difficult' because answering them often requires researchers to engage with deeper questions about what makes for good (effective, ethical, useful) research and what constitutes good (engaging, aesthetic) communication. Even for researchers who are not using fiction, these are helpful points to reflect on.

These difficult questions often have no easy or definitive answer. And it is not necessary to answer them all. However, we hope they will prompt engagement and reflection both prior to and during a research-fiction project, helping readers to clarify their objectives and achieve their aims and achieve success (whatever that might look like).

Reflective (and difficult) questions

- What would success look like for you? How will you know if you have achieved it?
- Do you have the skills to achieve your research-fiction aims? If not, how can you develop them or collaborate with others who do?
- What benefits and risks does fiction bring, compared to non-fictional representations of your data?
- How do/would you feel about your participants reading your research-based fiction?

Reflective exercise

Write an account – perhaps in the form of a fictional 'incident report' – describing a challenging situation or something going wrong in your own use of fiction in a research context. Include a description of the adverse event, the context in which it happened and its impact. You should also explain what actions you will take in response to the imagined incident. Alternatively, you may wish to explore such possibilities by writing a fictional letter of complaint from an imagined participant, stakeholder or colleague.

Whichever approach you take, use this imaginary scenario to consider ethical issues and difficult questions raised and make a plan to mitigate them.

PART III
Creating and sharing fiction

5

Crafting fictions: practical notes and creative prompts

> This chapter:
> - Considers the implications of decisions about who will (co-)create research fictions.
> - Shares some advice on creating an atmosphere conducive to creativity.
> - Offers a number of prompts to get you (and/or your collaborators) started on creating your own research-fiction.

Introduction

In this chapter, we offer some practical pointers on the process of creating research-fiction. We highlight some considerations about *who* produces research-based fiction, before discussing how to facilitate an environment and mindset conducive to creativity. We also provide some tips about overcoming inhibitions in creating fiction, and finally present a selection of prompts tailored to inspire research-based fictions.

How research-fiction is created: some practical considerations

A key decision for anyone wishing to create research-based fiction concerns *who* will create that fiction. As seen in the examples we have discussed, researchers can create fiction themselves, commission or collaborate with artists, writers or theatre practitioners, or can create contexts in which participants produce fiction. Of course, it is possible to combine these in various ways. Here, we review some practical considerations about such choices, and reflect on what might be involved in each form of fictional production.

Researchers creating research-based fiction themselves

Many works of fiction have been produced by researchers (examples highlighted in this book include Wolf 1992; Christensen 2009; Hecht 2017; Watson 2020; Toliver 2021), and researcher-authored work is particularly common where the fiction takes the form of a novel or short story. Researchers may choose to write fiction themselves because they wish to include autobiographical, reflexive elements which only *they* can write, and/or because they are deeply familiar with the data and ideas. In fact, Anna Banks comments that research-based fiction should *only* be written by researchers themselves because research is so personal, and only they will understand the research in sufficient depth to create fiction about it (Banks and Banks 1998: 18). Researchers may also choose to create fiction themselves because, for them, the research value of fiction lies in the *process*, rather than product, of creation, and the insights which fiction-writing can bring to data analysis (see Phillips and Kara 2021).

An important consideration for researchers considering writing their own research-fiction is whether they have the necessary skills to produce the type and quality of fiction they require (see Chapter 4). Another consideration is whether researchers have sufficient time and energy, given the wider requirements and priorities of their work, to create fiction.

Researchers who wish to create their own fiction may find useful insights in Ash Watson's (2022) reflections on writing sociological fiction and in Patricia Leavy's *Fiction as Research Practice* (2013), which provides an overview of 'fiction-based research' produced by a range of researchers. Leavy's more recent *Re/Invention: Methods of Social Fiction* (2022) also offers detailed guidance for researchers wishing to write 'social fiction' and includes illustrative excerpts from Leavy's own novels.

Commissioning (or collaborating with) artists and writers

An alternative strategy is that writers or artists may be commissioned to produce or contribute to works of fiction. This might entail commissioning fiction writers (Ryman 2010; Page 2012; Nesta 2015; Tipper and Gilman 2019; Satchwell et al 2020); comics artists (Hamdy and Nye 2017); animators (Satchwell et al 2020); or playwrights and screenwriters (Jones 2013; Lewando Hundt et al 2019).

In practical terms, commissioning a writer or artist will require funds to pay them fairly for their work and expertise – something that should be considered at the stage of research-planning. It might involve approaching an established writer, artist or theatre company directly or publicly advertising the commission. For university-based researchers, students or faculty members can also be a valuable source of expertise (for instance, both Hamdy et al and Satchwell et al worked with undergraduate artists). 'Artist in Residence' schemes – where an artist receives a fee from an institution in exchange for producing creative work – also provide a useful model; one example is the Creative Fellowships programme at Exeter University, UK, where artists working in various media are paired with researchers in diverse disciplines and generate creative outputs based on that research.

Commissioning a writer brings both challenges and opportunities. An experienced writer or artist will bring valuable specific craft skills to a project (Barone and Eisner 2012; Gibson 2021) and may enable a researcher to avoid stumbling into what Verónica Policarpo (2018) calls the 'no man's land' of research-based fiction which succeeds neither as academia nor as literary art.

A commissioned fiction-writer might also view a research topic with fresh eyes, offering new insights or clarity (perhaps even countering the risk of didacticism discussed earlier). However, this distance from the data can also bring difficulties: will the artist/writer be able to make the fiction 'ring true'? As a non-expert, will they be able to make sense of the data if it is complex or technical? Is it ethical for a commissioned artist to represent the experiences of a group that they are not part of (Phillips et al 2020: 42)? Where commissioned artists require access to interview data, researchers may need to reflect on whether (and how) the data should be anonymised or redacted, and whether participants have consented for their interviews to be used for such purposes (for example, Lafrenière and Cox 2013: 329). Finally, commissioning an artist can involve subtle negotiations, perhaps requiring a researcher to clarify their vision for the work, or relinquish some creative control over its final form (see, for example, Jones 2013).

Participant-produced fiction

As we have discussed, research participants might also be directly involved in the generation of fiction. Participants might co-create plays (Gembus 2018; Raynor 2019); write and refine short stories (Toliver 2021; Crockett Thomas 2022); make comics (McNicol 2019); or devise stories about imagined scenarios (Clarke and Braun 2019). Asking participants to create fictions might entail giving prompts to individual participants (Clarke and Braun 2019) or engaging more collaboratively with participants, whether in a group (Satchwell et al 2020) or a one-to-one setting (for example, Nägele et al 2018). (And, of course, commissioned professional writers can play a role in guiding this collaborative process, too [for example, Satchwell et al 2020; Rautio, 2022].) Participants can be recruited specifically to take part in a fiction-driven project (Toliver 2021; Crockett Thomas 2022) or researchers might work with an existing community group (Raynor 2019; Conrad 2023) or an extant writing/drama group (Gembus 2018).

How exactly the fiction is produced by a group may vary, but where participants produce fiction in workshops, this could include any combination of the following:

- participants discussing a piece of fiction they read prior to the workshop;
- warm-ups and icebreakers (in the form of written exercises or acting/improv games);
- writing individual responses to prompts;
- collective brainstorming to create fictional characters: for example, imagining their histories, personalities, likes and dislikes;
- collaboratively brainstorming responses to other prompts;
- participating in improvisational/acting prompts or role-play exercises;
- collaboratively generating and refining a story; and

- participants offering feedback about other participants' fiction (whether written outside of the group or generated during the workshop).

Researchers considering asking participants to (co-)create fiction should also consider whether and how this approach would work in the context of the communities they are working with and the topic they are exploring. Some useful resources for researchers planning to work with participants include Crockett Thomas' (2022) guide to participatory writing workshops with adults, and Satchwell et al's (2018) guide to collaborative story-writing with young people. Other resources include Matthew Salesses' *Craft in the Real World* (2021), which discusses the practicalities of creative writing workshops, with a focus on how workshops can foster an inclusive environment.

Facilitating creativity

Although preparing to create fiction entails making practical decisions about authorship/production and gaining familiarity with fictional techniques, preparation can also involve the more subtle process of facilitating an environment or mindset conducive to creativity, whether a researcher is writing alone or generating fiction in a group setting.

Where fiction is produced in workshops or groups, researchers will want to create a safe, comfortable atmosphere. This might involve admitting their own vulnerability (McMillan and McNicol 2021); providing assurances about anonymity; offering participants the opportunity to learn a skill through participation (Phillips and Kara 2021: 105); or clearly articulating how the fictional output/creative process could affect or benefit participants. Researchers, participants and/or workshop leaders will also need to negotiate ground rules about issues such as how the group will handle participants' disclosures about sensitive topics, as well as how much input a researcher will have, and how/whether critiques will be given on individuals' work. When researchers are working in collaboration with participants or commissioned artists, it is important that all involved hone their skills of offering encouragement and meaningful feedback. Constructive techniques include making positive observations alongside critical points, and framing feedback as *questions* rather than criticisms – for example, asking *why* a writer made particular choices (for example, Salesses 2021; Crockett Thomas 2022).

Participants new to fiction may also feel inhibited or hesitant about their own creative abilities, as may researchers who have not previously written creatively, and even seasoned fiction-writers can be vulnerable to self-doubt and distraction.

Writing mentors offer many strategies for overcoming inhibitions and dealing with distractions. Natalie Goldberg – whose books offer a Buddhist approach to the practice of creative writing (1986, 1991) – suggests that writers avoid pausing, correcting or self-consciously evaluating their work; instead, simply start to write and 'keep your hand moving' (1991: 2). Julia Cameron (2016) similarly encourages all artists to produce three handwritten pages soon after waking up, with no intention of showing them to anyone else – these 'morning pages' can become a daily practice enabling writers to become more fluent and creative. Stephen King advocates first writing 'with the door closed' (2010: 57), without any thought of an imagined reader coming into the room to read over one's shoulder, before later redrafting with the door open. Anne Lamott likewise encourages writers not to judge their initial work too harshly, and to embrace their inevitably 'shitty first draft' (2019: 21).

Warm-up exercises (done individually or in a group context) can be an excellent way to unleash creativity. Although the work generated through warm-ups *might* suggest ideas which writers choose to develop further (Gardner 1991), equally, the products of the exercises need not be shared with others, or even re-read by the writer. Most writing guides include warm-up ideas, and many prompts can be found online, but we offer some examples in Box 5.1.

Box 5.1: Warm-up exercises

- This warm-up exercise was devised by Natalie Goldberg. Write for ten minutes, beginning with the phrase 'I remember …' Explore whatever comes to mind (a single detailed memory or a series of recollections; distant or recent memories). If you come to a standstill, begin again with the phrase 'I remember …'.

    Take a short break and continue this exercise beginning with 'I don't remember …'.

This exercise is a good way to begin thinking creatively and attune to sensory and emotional details. Goldberg suggests it can open up 'the underbelly of your mind, the blank, dark spaces of your thoughts' (1991: 10) – a practice which could be useful for research-based fiction which aims to look beneath the surface or see data in new ways.

- Generate a list of five or six words (a workshop leader might provide the words, or a group could generate the words either at random or to fulfil categories such as an animal, a colour, a food, an emotion, a household object). Begin writing a story which incorporates the first word and, after a minute or two, find a way to include the next word. A workshop leader can announce when it is time to move on to the next word.

  In improv workshops, a similar exercise involves creating a story collaboratively, with participants each adding a single word at a time to the group's evolving story.

  These exercises push writers to make new connections and to think quickly – a good way to break through initial inhibitions. In both the written and improv versions, this can be a low-pressure way to practice generating a story – with conflicts, interesting characters and a satisfying ending – even when the content of that story is unpredictable.

- 'Fortunately/unfortunately' is a popular improv warm-up, although it would be equally possible to use this exercise as an individual writing prompt.

  Here, the group begins with a neutral prompt consisting of a single sentence, and each participant in the group adds a sentence to continue the story; the sentences must begin 'fortunately' and 'unfortunately' in turn, until the story resolves. The developments can be as realistic or light-hearted as the group wishes, but should aim to produce a coherent story.

  This exercise can loosen creative inhibitions, but also orients participants and writers to the twists, turns and conflicts that might shape a piece of fiction.

Prompts and exercises for creating fiction and thinking fictionally about research

Having decided who will be involved and taken some steps to 'warm up', you may feel ready to experiment with creating fiction yourself, or in collaboration with others. Although most generic creative-writing guides include prompts and exercises to stimulate ideas or hone particular skills, we focus here on ideas that may be especially relevant to research-fictions. We hope these pointers and prompts will open up ideas about linking research questions and data with fiction, inspire fictional thinking about research, and suggest ways you might begin and structure research-based stories. Although some of the points are specific to prose fiction, many are applicable to other fictional media, such as comics, performance, oral storytelling, animation or film. The prompts can be used to inspire 'finished' pieces (in conjunction with the more detailed craft resources outlined in the Further reading boxes), but they can also be used by researchers who wish to think creatively with fiction without any intent of sharing that fiction.

Reading a wide variety of fiction is an essential part of creating fiction; as Stephen King advises, 'If you want to be a writer, you must do two things above all others: read a lot and write a lot' (2010: 145). Therefore, within these prompts, we have highlighted pertinent and inspiring examples of fiction – both traditional and research-based – to illustrate techniques and concepts. Whether you are writing alone or working with research participants, reading existing works of fiction can spark ideas, provide models to emulate, and reveal what works (and what does not).

Fiction and im/possibilities: imagined worlds and unspoken taboos

As we noted in Chapter 2, fiction can bring to life entirely made-up, counterfactual, fantastical scenarios, which may seem far removed from real life. Inspiration for such non-realist stories can be found in published science fiction and fantasy; speculative and dystopian fiction; reimagined myths and fairy tales; and in fiction variously labelled as slipstream, magical realist, weird, uncanny, fabulist, absurd or surreal.

In Chapter 3 we discussed the use of speculative fiction in Toliver's (2021) work and Nesta's *Infectious Futures* project (2015). We also touched on Crockett Thomas' *Abolition Stories* (2022), Nägele et al's (2018) design fictions about medical care, and Rautio's stories of transformed human–animal relations (2022).

As we have noted, such fantastical storytelling might expose and interrogate current social realities, warn readers about future risks, or inspire thinking about other (better) ways of living.

However, utopian fictions about what H.G. Wells called 'ideal' societies can make for unengaging stories if they are *too* idealised (see also 'Shaping a story'). Accordingly, when Crockett Thomas' workshop participants created speculative stories, they based them around a 'novum' (a new thing or idea) which could transform society for the better, but they also incorporated an unintended and problematic consequence of the novum (Crockett Thomas 2022: 10).

Fantastical scenarios can be especially useful in dramatic and performative research. In Helen Cahill's (2010) participatory research about sexual health, she initially employed Forum Theatre techniques where participants acted out realistic interactions such as asking a partner to use a condom or discussing contraception with a doctor. However, Cahill found that participants were most uninhibited and engaged when the scenarios were instead surreal, funny and fantastical – for example, where they played the role of a talking penis or took the perspective of a 'cheeky condom' (2010: 160). When participants broke free of realism, they were able to engage in 're-storying' of their ordinary lives and see new possibilities.

In a similar vein, comedian and ethnographer Kate Fox suggests an improvisational comedy exercise for researchers, in which they explore 'what not to say during a conference paper' (Fox 2021: 163). Fox suggests this imaginative exercise can spark the 'joyous anarchy' of playing out what one would *never* say in real life, perhaps generating new ways of thinking and exposing social norms. Likewise, in short fiction, exploring taboo situations or desires can bring to the fore complex and contradictory feelings, which writer Alison Macleod observes are 'jet-fuel for stories; they immediately give the story the tension of opposing emotions and they are also, in all their messiness, particularly true to life' (Macleod 2013: 9; see also Douglas and Carless 2009 on exploring taboos through research-based fiction).

Prompts and ideas

- Try viewing your research question through the lens of fantastical or sci-fi tropes. How would aspects of your research

be impacted if time travel were possible, if extra-terrestrials made contact with earth, if a superhero intervened, or if scientific advances brought currently impossible things within reach? Tell a story about this.
- What inanimate objects and non-humans are relevant to your research topic? If they had agency or could speak, what would they do? What would they say?
- Through acting or writing, explore things you, as a researcher, or your research participants, could never say in your research context. What taboos exist? What would happen if they were violated? Can you find Fox's 'joyous anarchy' and Macleod's narrative 'jet fuel'?
- What would an ideal or utopian future look like in your research context? What 'novum' could transform the world? Write about how people would live in this new society – devise a scene, dialogue or descriptive passage, or another piece of writing. Next, imagine a problem that could be caused by this novum, and explore it through a protagonist who has to face this problem (based on Crockett Thomas [2022: 74], from an exercise devised by writer Michael Deerwater).

Getting under the skin of fictional characters

Many researchers are drawn to fiction because of its potential to allow readers to get 'under the skin' of a character – be that an entirely fictional individual, or a composite character who incorporates elements of several research participants.

Here, John Gardner's concept of 'psychic distance' is particularly relevant. Gardner illustrates this concept with the following example:

1. It was winter of the year 1853. A large man stepped out of a doorway.
2. Henry Warburton had never much cared for snow storms.
3. Henry hated snowstorms.
4. God how he hated these damn snowstorms.
5. Snow. Under your collar, down inside your shoes freezing and plugging up your miserable soul ... (1991: 111)

For any researcher aiming to get under the skin (or step into the cold, wet shoes) of a character, an attention to psychic distance is essential. Effective fiction will move judiciously between Gardner's levels of psychic distance, much as films contain both wide and close-up shots (although Gardner cautions against sudden, jarring shifts). And, as Ash Watson notes, sociological fiction particularly benefits from controlled 'zooming out and in again' between a character's internal experience and 'a macro view of the scene as societal in scale' (2022: 345).

An important aspect of close psychic distance is the evocation of sensory detail – in just a few words, we *feel* the oppression of Henry Warburton's chilled neck and feet. Recall also Alan Lightman's description of the smell of linseed and the cracking voice of a grandfather (Chapter 1), or A.S. Fields' depiction of the 'never ending slow burn' of urinary tract infection pain, like a veld fire charring the mountains (Chapter 3). For Gardner (1991), such descriptions contribute to the creation of the 'fictional dream' – the rich details which immerse a reader in a fictional world, rendering a piece of fiction believable. And, for many writers of research-fiction, these specific and sensory details are an integral part of conveying experience and giving meaning to the events depicted (Leavy 2022; Watson 2022).

Some scenes offer a wealth of sensory possibilities – a hospital, a restaurant or a bustling city are all replete with specific, sensory detail – but grounding any experience in the senses can make it visceral and engaging. Prose writers can also intensify emotional reactions by adding a sensory element – for instance, how does anger/excitement/anticipation *feel* in the body?

Prompts and ideas

- Imagine a short scene, a moment or experience inspired by your research topic and describe it through Gardner's five levels of psychic distance: beginning as an external observer and moving closer, finally stepping into the shoes of a character to feel what they feel.
- A simple way to create sensory descriptions is to focus on three senses (a technique often attributed to Gustave Flaubert) – more than three can be used, although this risks overwhelming the

reader. Take a moment you wish to explore – an imagined scenario, or an event experienced by a research participant – and write about it, alert to what the character might taste, see, hear, feel or smell (using at least three of these senses). Allow yourself to make connections and expand on these observations: what emotions and memories do they trigger? Consider the absence of senses: what can they *not* see/hear/smell/taste/feel?

The heft of metaphors

Metaphors (which state that two things *are* the same) and similes (which suggest two disparate things are *alike*), add potency to fictional worlds. Metaphors can add layers of meaning, echo themes in a story, and amplify the emotions and conflicts experienced by characters. They can also be a way to 'show' rather than 'tell' ideas.

When metaphors ground abstract ideas in physical experience, they can bring prose vividly to life, allowing the reader to viscerally experience a fictional world. Will Storr notes that even in the simple phrase, 'a rough day', we '*feel* the heft and strain of the shouldering, we *touch* the abrasiveness of the day' (2020: 45, emphasis in original). Likewise, poet Jane Hirshfield observes (in an animated TED Talk):

> Metaphors are a way to talk about one thing by describing something else. That may seem roundabout, but it's not. Seeing and hearing and tasting are how we know anything first. ... Metaphors think with the imagination *and* the senses. The hot chili peppers in them explode in the mouth and the mind. (Hirshfield 2012 at 0:36, emphasis in original)

While fiction authors are often encouraged to be wary of well-used comparisons, so-called 'dead' metaphors might also be used with powerful effect to create fantastical scenarios: in her story collection, *Roar* (2019), Cecelia Ahern reinvigorates these ordinary figures of speech by using them as the basis for surreal short fiction. In one story, a 'trophy wife' is, quite literally, kept on a shelf, where she is admired and intermittently dusted. In another, a woman has a mortifying experience in a meeting and wishes the ground would swallow her up, only to find that the floor does literally open, allowing her to disappear underneath it (see also the section on 'Fiction and im/possibilities').

Metaphors can be crafted by researchers, but they may also emerge from the data – particularly if interview participants employ metaphors to speak about their experiences. This can be a powerful way to create a new story which resonates with participants' meanings. In our own work, when Becky wrote short fictions based on Leah and colleagues' qualitative research about egg donation, participants' use of metaphor inspired the setting of some stories. For instance, interviewees sometimes compared egg donation to giving away clothes to a charity shop, using this metaphor to express two possibilities: (1) that these two actions were similar; or (2) that they were utterly incomparable. (Specifically, one interviewee suggested that just as she would not give away a coat and follow up to ensure that the buyer was wearing it 'correctly', so would it be unreasonable to donate eggs expecting to know who would receive them. Another participant, however, argued that donating gametes was a profound decision which was *nothing like* the trivial act of giving away old clothes.) This metaphor informed the backdrop for one story in which two characters clear out a room and set aside unwanted items to donate to charity while playing out these questions about the meaning of egg donation: does donation necessarily end any connection between the donor and the eggs (as it would in the case of a donated coat)? How appropriate is it to wonder about what became of a donation (Tipper and Gilman 2019)?

Metaphors, then, can arise from social research participants' own words. However, they might also be found in academic discussions of a research topic. For example, Emily Martin's (1991) analysis of anatomy textbooks demonstrates how gendered fairy tale tropes often shape the descriptions of eggs and sperm, depicted respectively as damsels in distress and heroic warriors. And, as Laurel Richardson remarks, social researchers also use metaphor to construct the authority of their knowledge claims (1997a: 37) – for instance, terms such as 'fieldwork', 'triangulation' or data 'mining' evoke images of research as physical, visual work, perhaps akin to construction. But what would it mean to imagine academic theory not as a 'building block', and instead as a feather (Richardson 1997a: 44), or to conceive of research as a process of crystallisation (Richardson and St. Pierre 2005: 963)?

Prompts and ideas

- What metaphors are used about your research topic? What metaphors appear in the theory you draw on? If you are working with research participants, what metaphors do they use? What additional concrete, sensory metaphors or similes do *you* think describe experiences, emotions or events you have experienced through your research?
- Use one of these metaphors in any way you choose. The metaphor could provide a starting point for a story, or it could inspire the incidental backdrop to a fictional scene or dialogue. Or you could create a fantastical Ahern-style fiction in which the metaphor 'comes to life'.

Shaping a story: characters, desire, conflict, dilemma and change

Some researchers interested in fiction will already have ideas and issues they wish to explore through stories, and may be mainly concerned with how to craft and structure those stories. Returning to the ideas we highlighted in Chapter 1, we suggest that one way to do this effectively is to focus on the interconnected elements which power fictional stories: characters who have goals, who face conflicts and make choices, and stories which express change.

Desire is a driving force in fiction – elegantly summed up in Kurt Vonnegut's oft-cited maxim that every character in a story should *want* something, even if it is just a glass of water. As fictional characters seek to achieve goals, they face obstacles and problems which prevent them from getting what they desire. Such problems give rise to conflicts, which are the essence of much compelling fiction. John Gardner explains:

> Certain forces, within and outside the character, must press him toward a certain course of action, while other

forces, both within and outside, must exert strong pressure against that course of action. Both pressures must come not only from outside the character but also from within him, because otherwise the conflict involves no doubt, no moral choice, and as a result can have no profound meaning. (Gardner 1991: 187)

Cross-cutting characters' desires and conflicts is the force of *change*: 'any good story is about when something, perhaps everything, changed' notes editor Ra Page (2012: 1). Sudden changes can trigger fictional action (as characters seek to overcome or understand those changes), and the obstacles a character faces in a story will likely change them. In fact, Will Storr specifically advises writers with a story idea (such as a fantastical 'what if' scenario) to build their story around the specific character who would be 'maximally changed' by that event (2020: 113). Whether the character undergoes a reversal of fortunes (peripeteia), or a smaller but profound shift in perception, a changed character will emerge from the story a different person from who they were at the story's beginning. (Although occasionally, stories can focus on the *impossibility* of change, and on characters who are 'pinned in stasis' [Tomlinson 2006: 27], or who fail or refuse to change [Salesses 2021: 160]).

Identifying change, desire and conflict provides some starting points for crafting engaging stories, although writers producing longer works of fiction will probably want to explore more detailed plotting advice about *how* exactly these conflicts usually unfold in novellas (for example, Warner 2021), novels (for example, Gardner 1991) or scripts (for example, McKee 1997).

Many of these points are illustrated elegantly in the graphic novel *Lissa* (discussed in Chapter 3), in which anthropologists Hamdy and Nye explored questions of medical decision-making in Egyptian and US cultures. *Lissa*'s characters face multiple overlapping challenges and 'external pressures'. For instance, both Anna and Layla's families navigate the critical ill-health of a family member. Both families face difficulties in obtaining medical care: Anna's US treatment is costly, while Layla's father's access to care in Egypt is hindered by political corruption and unrest. Both families also face conflicting pressures about medical decisions – a kidney transplant in Layla's father's case, and a preventive mastectomy in Anna's case. Such pressures are interpersonal, environmental and circumstantial, but the characters also face numerous *internal* conflicts: they must decide what is the right course of action. This means weighing moral, relational and religious questions about *who they are* (what kind of daughter, what kind of Muslim); how they should face mortality; and how to live with risk.

These conflicts are central to the story. As a result, the two main characters each face a 'true dilemma' (McKee 1997: 304): a conflicting choice between the 'lesser of two evils' where *no* unproblematic option exists. Anna must choose either to undergo an irreversible, life-changing operation (against the advice of her father and best friend) or live with the risk of cancer. Meanwhile, Layla is trapped between watching her father suffer or persuading him to violate his beliefs by accepting a kidney transplant. As they navigate these conflicts and confront the choice of this dilemma, the characters' lives change irrevocably.

Prompts and ideas

- What key desires and goals drive research participants, or the characters in a prospective research-based fiction? (Note, those desires might be as simple as staying healthy and alive, as in the Nesta stories or *Lissa*.) What obstacles stand in their way? How do they overcome them?
- In your research area, what external forces impact people's lives? What internal conflicts could arise? What impossible choices and dilemmas do people face? If you are inventing a new story, outline the internal and external conflicts your character would experience in a fictional situation.
(Remember that these conflicts and dilemmas can be small and mundane, as well as profound and life-changing: whenever a character's internal and external pressures clash, this conflict can produce an engaging story. And even ordinary, but irresolvable, decisions can present meaningful dilemmas.)
- Write a short piece in which a character, or their world (inspired by your research topic), changes fundamentally. If you are working with narrative data, look at how participants

discuss their own experiences of turning points, revelations or broad social change. If you are working with statistics, you may draw inspiration from changes in patterns of data over time or from anomalies within the dataset.

(Again, these changes do not have to be grand in scale – a shift in perception, a small realisation, or a decision to act differently can all create meaningful stories.)

Familiar forms and borrowed plots

Drawing on existing stories can provide much inspiration for researchers. Using a familiar story as a model can be a simple way to approach issues of structure: a plot has been established, and conflicts, climaxes and potential resolutions are identified. Reusing plots is a traditional means of storytelling, employed by Shakespeare and Dostoyevsky (Gardner 1991: 56). Many well-known fictions retell existing stories – famous examples include Zadie Smith's novel *On Beauty*, based on E.M. Forster's *Howard's End*; the musical *West Side Story*, based on *Romeo and Juliet*; and Posy Simmonds' graphic novel *Tamara Drewe*, based on Thomas Hardy's *Far From the Madding Crowd*.

Some stories – myths, folktales and fairy tales in particular – have been refined and tested over generations. Such stories are often recognisable to most members of a culture. Consequently, they offer a familiar, accessible format through which to tell *new* stories. For example, Lord et al (2023) used fairy tale characters to encourage people to think differently about sustainability and climate change, and Andrew Simms (2017) invited writers, academics and experts to explore contemporary social and environmental crises through retold folk tales.

A related way of using existing structures is through 'hermit crab' stories – fictions which occupy the shell of incongruous, often non-fictional, formats. Such stories can be entertaining, and are often emotionally powerful. Some excellent (online) examples include Dan Brotzel's 'Active and Passive Voice' (2019), a short story of lost love in the style of a grammar manual, and Mary South's 'Frequently Asked Questions about Your Craniotomy' (2020), a fiction inspired by medical information leaflets. Following in this tradition, researchers could explore the possibilities of creating hermit crab pieces that resonate with their research – for instance, a scientific protocol might provide a basis for a story; or a social research study might invite participants to invent fictional answers to documents they are accustomed to completing, such as benefit applications or medical history forms.

Prompts and ideas

- To create hermit crab stories, start by making a list of written formats related to your research area. These could include: an advice column, an instruction manual, a dictionary or encyclopaedia entry, a job application, a shopping list, a recipe, a newspaper report (or another form relevant to your research). Write a story that inhabits (or is inspired by) one of these styles.
- Do participants in your research compare their experiences to any existing story or genre? For example, Leah has recently interviewed donor-conceived people about their experiences of using direct-to-consumer genetic testing. Several likened their stories (which often involved unexpected discoveries of genetic relatives) to those shared on the talk show *The Jeremy Kyle Show* or to the plots of soap operas. Participants' analogies can provide inspiration for the form or setting for a research-inspired story.
- Use a familiar folk tale (or its characters) to tell a new story related to your research. Alternatively, tell a research-related story in the form of the hero's journey (as North's [2017] participants did), or based around another traditional story structure (discussed in Chapter 1).

Point of view

In creating fiction, writers must make decisions about who the narrator(s) will be, and how exactly they will address the audience. In research-fictions, these considerations open up distinctive possibilities.

In prose fiction, the point of view is often the first person (I), or the third person (she/he/they). First-person stories can be engaging (although fictional first-person stories by researchers may become problematic if they could be misinterpreted by readers as a 'real' participant's story [for example, Christensen 2012; Leavy 2013: 46]). Third-person stories can take various degrees of distance – most commonly, in the third-person limited view, a writer refers to characters as she/he but also has access to characters' inner worlds. The third-person omniscient view grants a writer access to the thoughts and feelings of *all* characters (although excessive 'head-hopping' between characters can become confusing or overwhelming for readers).

Prose can also be written in the second person (you). Such fictions might address particular individuals (see also Phillips and Kara 2021: 29–30), perhaps through fictional letters – as in epistolary novels from Bram Stoker's *Dracula* to Lionel Shriver's *We Need to Talk about Kevin*. For instance, our own short stories about egg donation included one story in the form of a letter from a fictional egg donor to the recipient of her eggs (Tipper and Gilman 2019). An addressee can also be more abstract – for instance, a future self, a concept (such as death, an illness or disability) or a fictional being (see Chapter 3). However, in some cases, the second person is used not to address a particular individual, but to tell stories where the narrator, author and/or the reader become ambiguously intertwined, or where readers are invited to take on the role of the protagonist. Such second-person stories are often surprising, engaging and (productively) disorienting (for example, Keen 2006: 225; Warner 2021: 114–115). Short fiction often uses the second person to good effect, as in Kate Clanchy's 'Animal, Vegetable', which begins: 'In this story, you have a particular friend. You've known her a long time – since college at least ... she's your high-achieving friend ... a bit more glamorous than you, too: a size down in jeans. ... No spots, no fillings' (Clanchy 2015: 157). More unusual is the use of the first-person plural (we), although one striking prose example is Annie Ernaux's creative memoir *The Years* (2017), where at times the story seems to be told by a whole generation of similarly situated characters.

Dramatic or theatrical performances can equally explore these possibilities. Ethnodramas often take the form of fictionalised monologues (Saldaña 2005), exemplified in Eve Ensler's interview-based play *The Vagina Monologues* (1998) – monologues might be delivered in the first person, or in the second person if the monologue is addressed to an imagined interlocutor. Actors, or narrators, can also break the fourth wall to address 'you', the audience, directly. Choruses offer distinctive potentials for dramatic performances – in Ancient Greek drama, a chorus traditionally explained or passed comment on the action; however, in contemporary theatre, choruses have been used creatively to represent the voices of multiple individuals (for example, Paula Vogel's 2018 play *How I Learned to Drive*), or even omniscient beings (for example, Sarah Ruhl's 2008 *Eurydice*).

Researchers may find that taking a particular point of view communicates their research effectively, or that exploring (or asking participants to explore) different points of view can be a productive means to explore ideas and think in new ways about familiar experiences.

Prompts and ideas

- Try writing about your own experience (as a researcher, or as a research participant) in both the first and third person. Reflect on what each point of view affords.
- In your research context, what letters could be written to real or imagined others? Write a letter, or imagine a dialogue, in which you address these others. What would you like to say? (And what might they say in reply?)
- Are there 'we' stories to tell about your research? What groups of people could speak with a single voice? Whom would they address?
- An omniscient perspective or narrator in a story might have access to all the characters' perspectives or know what the future holds – even if you are sceptical of a 'view from nowhere', you could explore what an omniscient point of view, or a narrator situated outside the action, brings to your fiction.

Speaking fictionally: real speech and imagined dialogues

Well-crafted dialogue is an important part of much prose and many comics and graphic novels, while of course screenplays and scripts consist almost entirely of dialogue. Depending on a researcher's approach, there are various strategies for developing fictional dialogue.

For researchers who have access to interview transcripts, writing fictional speech might seem straightforward. Transcripts offer the authentic details which many verbatim theatre practitioners seek to preserve, enabling them to represent the tone and speech patterning of 'real people' and those everyday hesitations, stutters and mispronunciations which fiction writers commonly elide (Shah and Greer 2018). While true verbatim theatre uses only original words and tones of speech, writers might also employ narrative creativity in the selection and curation of these extracts, as well as in casting and set design (Hammond and Steward 2012).

However, some researchers converting transcripts to fiction may decide to cull many of the 'real' words. For instance, Johnny Saldaña advises researchers producing ethnodramas based on interview transcripts to create dialogue which *resembles* participants' real words, but (as he succinctly puts it) 'with all the boring parts taken out' (2005: 16).

Certainly, from the point of view of many fiction writers, verbatim transcripts alone might not be enough to create effective dialogue: they suggest that fictional dialogue should be more dramatic, pointed and condensed than real-world words. As Anne Lamott comments, good writing is not about 'reproducing actual speech' but instead 'putting down on paper your *sense of how the characters speak*' (Lamott 2019: 65; italics ours). Fiction writers also emphasise that dialogue needs to perform multiple functions; as Will Storr advises, fictional dialogue should 'both sound true and writhe with meaning' (2020: 132). Specifically, dialogue should convey characters' personalities and contribute to the unfolding story – through dialogue, playwrights 'not only advance the action, [but also] reveal character *re*action' (Saldaña 2005: 25). Additionally, dialogue often reveals subtexts or unspoken issues, desires and conflicts; in the words of Robert McKee, dialogue is rarely about 'what it seems to be about' (McKee 1997: 388–389).

On a practical note, in fictional prose dialogue, less is often more; for instance, many contemporary writers favour 'said' over more colourful dialogue tags such as 'exclaimed', 'queried' or 'bellowed' (although such tags are sometimes stylistically appropriate). It is also useful to remember that you might not need a dialogue tag at all if the speaker is obvious and if the tone of the speech is evident (for instance, tags such as 'concurred', 'responded' or 'he said angrily' might be superfluous if this is clear from the dialogue itself).

Prompts and ideas

- Tim Tomlinson notes that *arguments* are an effective way to practice writing engaging dialogue: 'as long as characters are in disagreement, you have conflict, and if you have conflict you have a scene, since the dramatic tension will be created by the questions in the reader's mind: How will character A attempt to impose her will on character B?' (2006: 48).
  Create a dialogue in which two characters clash in this way. Every statement from one must be met with disagreement from the other. Tomlinson notes that Monty Python's 'Argument Clinic' sketch can provide inspiration for this exercise!
  You might wish to do this exercise in conjunction with your reflections on conflict (see the section on 'Shaping a story'). And if you are working with transcripts, you could juxtapose interviewees' verbatim comments to create such an argument.
- If you are working with interview transcripts, explore their subtexts and omissions. Create a fictional paratext in which you imagine what was *not* said in answer to the interviewer's questions, or imagine what the interviewee might have been implying, thinking or holding back. You could do this by beginning with the statement 'What I *didn't* say was …'.
- Recorded delivery is a verbatim theatre method pioneered by Alecky Blythe (2014) in which actors simultaneously listen to and reproduce selected recorded conversations. Try this technique with a selection of interview extracts, attempting to preserve the tone and idiosyncrasies of the original. If you have consent to share audio data, ask someone else to voice the words of another participant. What happens when these performances are brought into dialogue with one another?

The power of brevity: very short stories

Ernest Hemingway is often credited with writing the shortest of short stories: 'For sale: baby shoes, never worn.' Very short fiction can, of course, be longer than Hemingway's six words – stories of exactly 100 words are known as 'drabbles', while 'flash fiction' is a broader term which generally refers to 250–1,500-word stories. Published flash fiction is readily found in online literary journals such as *100 Word Story*; *Smokelong Quarterly* (featuring bold, sometimes experimental pieces); *Flash Fiction Online* (traditional stories, as well as fantasy and sci-fi); and *Flashback Fiction* (historically inspired stories). These stories can be evocative, puzzling, humorous, pithy or moving, and they offer some inspiring possibilities for research-based fiction.

Such stories are not necessarily easy to write, but they can allow a writer to distil ideas or find new perspectives on a familiar topic. Flash fiction (in contrast to short stories or novels) can also feel less daunting to new writers. In a research context, very short participant-produced stories could be analysed as data, or be used as a jumping off point for further discussion. Creating a series of flash fictions can also offer one way to explore diverse perspectives (see the section on 'Polyvocality and multiple stories').

Inspired by the six-word story, writer and researcher Kate North invited parents of children with autism to write 15-word stories depicting their 'ideal' experience of Autism Spectrum Disorder care. She asked participants to break the story into three sections of up to five words each: 'a beginning that set up a goal; a middle that stated how obstacles would be overcome for the goal to be achieved; and an ideal ending or outcome' (North 2017: np). One participant's story read: 'Dreams of American freight trains. Travels, watches, learns, asks questions. Grows up, drives that train.'

As North shows, one starting point is to focus on overcoming a problem. You might also try to step into 'the middle' of the action (Gaffney 2013). Or begin with a striking or unusual image, or a moment of change. Flash fiction is also an excellent way to explore fantastical scenarios or surreal ideas, allowing a writer to jump straight into the logic of another universe (Hershman 2013; Marek 2013).

Prompts and ideas

- Write – or ask participants to write – a story with a specific word count (six, or 50, or 100, or another number of your choice).

- Flash-fiction writer Tania Hershman suggests setting a timer before beginning to write in order to focus fully: 'you are going to write *knowing* that after twenty or thirty minutes you will have a complete flash story' (2013: 174, emphasis in original).
- If you have written a longer story, see if you can make it half as long, or reduce it to a few hundred words (Gaffney 2013; Le Guin 2015). This exercise can strengthen a story by rendering certain aspects unsaid or implied, and can also reveal the most powerful or important ideas within a piece of fiction.

Polyvocality and multiple stories

A well-crafted piece of fiction can convey a single character's psyche and inner life with depth and subtlety – perhaps through a novel (for example, Watson 2020) or a short story (for example, Christensen 2009). However, there is a risk that a single story might appear to be the *only* story that can be told about the data (Inckle 2010) or could shut down alternative voices (Cahill 2010: 172). For some researchers, fiction which instead embraces multiple perspectives, stories or characters enables them to create a polyphonous, open-ended representation of their research or data, which may be particularly suited to their purposes or their theoretical stance (for example, Banks and Banks 1998; Frank 2000).

One way of producing polyvocal fictions is to write several short (or flash) stories, perhaps from multiple perspectives. Marcelo Diversi (1998) wrote a series of 14 short fictions to convey the lives of Brazilian street children he encountered during his research. In our own collaboration, we produced six short stories about egg donors in the UK; each story follows a character who comes to donate eggs through a distinct set of circumstances. The six stories explore possible outcomes and ways that different donors might understand their experiences (Tipper and Gilman 2019, 2022). Tobias Hecht's 'Denial' stories (Chapter 3) maintain one point of view (that of 'the visitor') but they also show how a series of discrete but related fictions can offer a view of research that resembles (depending on one's metaphor of choice) a mosaic, a patchwork, a kaleidoscopic view, or an array of photographic snapshots.

Another striking model is anthropologist Margery Wolf's *Tale Thrice Told* (1992), a three-part exploration of an incident from her ethnographic research in Taiwan. Wolf relates the incident in three ways: (1) as a fictional short story; (2) in an academic article; and (3) through her unfiltered fieldnotes. Although only one of Wolf's perspectives is fictional, together they offer a fascinating exploration of the possibilities – and limitations – of viewing research experiences through multiple lenses.

Frequently, theatrical fictions employ multivocal presentations to represent diverse perspectives – performances might take the form of parallel or serial monologues, or may present a fictional story which literally brings them into dialogue with one another (for example, Saldaña 2005). Eve Ensler's *The Vagina Monologues* is one famous example. In Chapter 3, we discussed the verbatim play *Passing On* – which presents the voices of patients and various medical professionals – and Harvey Humphrey's play *AS IS* – which features the sometimes conflicting viewpoints of LGBTI activists. The result can resemble a 'collage' of diverse voices (Shah and Greer 2018: 65).

Prompts and ideas

- Dramatic workshops (which may include research participants or be inspired by research data) are well-placed to explore multiple perspectives. For instance, in Forum Theatre exercises, participants portray an oppressive situation and explore, through role-play, different possibilities for resisting the oppression. Throughout the exercise, different participants/actors (in Boal's terms, 'spect-actors') can step in to play the role of *any* of the characters in the scenario. This means a participant might experience playing the roles of both 'oppressor' *and* 'oppressed'. The representations of all the scenario's characters are likely to become complex and nuanced as different actors portray them and navigate new iterations of the scenario (Boal 2002: 243–245, 221).
- In writing, describe the same research-related event from multiple perspectives (for instance, a medical appointment seen

through the eyes of doctor, a parent and a child). This could be done as an individual writing exercise, or in a group participants could choose, or be assigned, a perspective to write from.
- If you, or your participants, have generated fiction which represents various perspectives, reflect on them as a whole. What contradictions, omissions or resonances do you see?

6

Next steps: sharing research-fictions

This chapter:
- Explores various routes through which research-fiction can be shared, via publication and performance.
- Considers how different routes for publication and performance shape the reach and accessibility of the work.
- Provides a list of potential publishers of research-fiction.
- Prompts readers to consider whether new fora for research-fiction are desirable in their research context or discipline.

Introduction

For some researchers, the primary value of fiction lies in the *process* of creating and/or responding to stories. However, for many others, finished fictional *products* will constitute important outputs which they wish to share with others beyond their immediate colleagues and collaborators. Potential audiences with whom such pieces might be shared include other researchers and academics (both within and beyond the researcher's discipline), stakeholders whose professional or personal experiences relate to the research topic, policy makers (or others with the power to instigate change) and wider publics.

In order to reach their intended audience(s), researchers must consider carefully where and how they will publish or otherwise share the fictions they create, co-create or commission. As Gibson (2021) highlights, and as we discussed in Chapter 4, despite an emphasis on fiction as a method of engaging publics beyond the academy, research-fictions (particularly when published as texts rather than performed) are often shared in academic journals (particularly those with a methodological focus). This is not necessarily a bad thing and is indicative of the constraints and expectations of academic researchers. However, Gibson's critique points to the importance of aligning fora for publication and performance with research-fiction objectives and rationales. Objectives may, of course, be multiple and so too audiences and strategies for dissemination.

In this short chapter, we outline various approaches to publication and performance used by researchers who employ fiction in their work, and discuss some of the benefits and limitations of each.

Sharing through performance

In the case of fictional drama, sharing the work often involves performance. In such cases, researchers will need to decide where the performance(s) will be staged/filmed, including whether they will be accessed online or in-person, and how they will gather their audience (by invitation or advertisement). For example, in the case of *Passing On*, the researchers invited tailored audiences of medical students and people with a connection to the geographical area of the study to attend performances (Lewando Hundt et al 2019). Humphrey and colleagues describe their decision not to advertise their live performance of *AS IS* via academic routes, instead promoting it via personal networks, social media and local stakeholder communities (in this case, Scottish and particular Glasgow-based LGBTQIA+ groups) in order to gather a supportive audience for their work (Humphrey et al 2023).

Such decisions will have implications for who is included (or not) in, and thus impacted by, any performance. This is something which Humphrey and colleagues reflected on post-performance, particularly mindful of how their decision to perform the play to a live audience during the COVID-19 pandemic would have (despite the requirement to wear masks) excluded or deterred some from attending. They describe the decision to film and later share the recording (both at a planned screening and also on request) as an 'imperfect solution' (Humphrey et al 2023: 11).

Performances need not be theatrical. Films are a route through which research-based fictions can be performed in multiple locations, often with greater realism than is possible in theatre. Kip Jones' award-winning short film, *Rufus Stone* (discussed in Chapter 3) is one of very few professionally produced research-inspired fictional films we are aware of (perhaps indicative of the costs of this method of dissemination). While resource-intensive, the film was subsequently used for multiple screenings and community-based workshops, creating what the researchers call the 'long tail' of effective research engagement and impact (Fenge et al 2018: 52).

A lower cost method of performance is to read short pieces of fiction aloud to an audience. For example, Douglas and Carless wrote short fiction about sexual harassment in elite sport, and shared this with relevant audiences, including groups of sports science students (Douglas and Carless 2009). Fiction might also be shared at academic conferences (Douglas and Carless 2009; Watson 2011), and increasingly, academic conferences are featuring 'creative' and 'artistic' outputs.

Sharing through websites, booklets and self-publication

Self-publication, particularly online, is a common method of dissemination for research-fiction.

The internet provides ample opportunities for researchers to share outputs with a wide range of audiences, often at zero or low cost. Various platforms can be used. Researchers may choose to set up a dedicated website to host research-based fictional outputs relating to a particular project – whether written prose, comics or audio-visual material (Satchwell et al 2020). Alternatively, fictional outputs can be shared via existing platforms embedded within institutional websites. For example, audio recordings of short stories can be released as podcasts. Short stories can be shared on existing or project-specific blogs. Audio stories, animations, films or performance recordings can be made available (and/or live-streamed) via video hosting platforms, such as YouTube or Vimeo.

In many of the examples we have discussed in this book, researchers have shared short research-based fiction via downloadable or printed booklets (Nesta 2015; Sou and Cei Douglas 2019; Tipper and Gilman 2019, 2022; Crockett Thomas 2022). If physical copies are printed, they can also be distributed directly and indirectly (via charities, professional bodies and other organisations) to target audiences.

For researchers who wish to self-publish longer works of fiction, such as novels, Patricia Leavy discusses the practicalities of this route in some detail (2022: 194–196). There are a number of (more or less reputable) companies who will offer services such as typesetting, editing, design and printing, for an upfront cost, although this can be substantial – Haurant (2022), cites self-published novelist Paul Illett's estimate of £4,000 to produce a professional-quality book.

In short, self-publication can be an effective way of making fictional outputs widely accessible, circumventing the requirements and timescales of academic or literary publishers. However, it can be costly and does also depend on how effectively the researcher can publicise their work, allowing interested readers to find it.

Literary publishers

Short research-based fiction (or creative non-fiction) might also find a home in literary magazines. Many literary magazines publish short fiction and creative non-fiction, and some also accept dramatic scripts and comics. Hundreds of literary magazines exist, both online and in print – for instance, *The New Yorker* and *Granta* are two of the most high-profile global publishers of fiction and creative non-fiction, although both have a forbidding acceptance rate. One useful resource for writers submitting to literary magazines is Duotrope – a paid subscription website with a searchable database of publications and their acceptance rates, which might enable researchers to identify literary magazines which would be a good fit for their research-based fiction. However, many literary magazines do not accept previously published work, so this route may not be appropriate for fiction which has already appeared in an academic journal or on a university website. Additionally, while some literary magazines are free to read online, if researchers publish in literary magazines which are only available to purchase, they may need to consider whether this contravenes funding requirements to make their research products open access.

In some instances, mainstream publishers and literary presses may be open to publishing research-based short story anthologies/collections or novels – for example, although the Comma Press *Science into Fiction* anthologies were commissioned and instigated by the publisher and not by researchers, they do show how research-based fiction can be presented and marketed by a literary publisher.

Academic publishers and professional magazines

Some conventional academic journals (and academic publishers) accept fictional, or otherwise creative, submissions. However, as Patricia Leavy (2022: 193) notes, even if academic publishers do not state they will consider fiction submissions, they may be open to considering such work if queried. Journals or book publishers with a focus on interdisciplinarity or creative research methods may be a particularly open to fictional work – S.R. Toliver's *Endarkened Storywork* was published by Routledge, as a hybrid fictional-academic text in the book series *Futures of Data Analysis in Qualitative Research*. Box 6.1 lists some academic journals that accept fictional submissions.

Additionally, publications produced by stakeholder organisations (such as charities, businesses or community groups) linked to the topic of the research may be interested in relevant research-based fiction. For instance, some of the short stories about egg donors that resulted from our own collaboration were subsequently published in the *Journal of Fertility Counselling*, a publication for professional counsellors.

Box 6.1: Some outlets and resources for research-based fiction

Academic journals

These academic (or primarily scholarly) journals publish conventional research articles but also welcome fictional submissions. Of course, we recommend that potential contributors consult the journal's own instructions for authors before submitting.

Aethlon: The Journal of Sport Literature (East Tennessee State University)
American Journal of Nursing (Lippincott, Williams & Wilkins)
Animal Studies Journal (University of Wollongong)
Antennae: The Journal of Nature in Visual Culture
Anthropology and Humanism (Wiley)
Art/Research International: A Trans-disciplinary Journal (University of Alberta)
Early American Studies: An Interdisciplinary Journal (University of Pennsylvania Press)
Entanglements: Experiments in Multimodal Ethnography (note: this online journal published its final issue in 2022 but is included here for reference)
Feminist Review (SAGE)
Hektoen International: A Journal of Medical Humanities (Hektoen Institute of Medicine)
Intima: A Journal of Narrative Medicine
ISLE: Interdisciplinary Studies of Literature and Environment (Oxford University Press)
Journal of Latina Critical Feminism
Journal of Medical Humanities (Springer)
KRITIKE: An Online Journal of Philosophy (University of Santo Tomas)
Practicing Anthropology (Society for Applied Anthropology)
Qualitative Inquiry (SAGE)
Revenant: Critical and Creative Studies of the Supernatural
The Sociological Review (SAGE)

Literary magazines with a focus on research

As we have noted, short research-based fiction could be submitted to mainstream literary magazines. However, the following literary publications might be of particular interest to researchers since they explicitly seek creative work that relates to research or academia.

- *AcademFic: A Journal of Fiction by Academics* (Butler University and PALNI Press). This online, open-access journal publishes short stories, reviews of fiction and essays about the use of fiction by academics.

- *Ars Medica: A Journal of Medicine, the Arts, and Humanities*. Publishes fiction, creative non-fiction and visual art exploring the interface between medicine and the arts.
- *Lablit: The Culture of Science in Fiction and Fact*. This website is dedicated to fiction about scientists and scientific work.
- *Otherwise*. An online magazine which publishes short fiction, creative non-fiction, visual essays, and short graphic novels or comics based on ethnographic research.
- *SoFi Zine*. An online zine featuring a range of creative outputs arising from social science research (edited by Ash Watson).
- *The Woodward Review* (Wayne State University). This journal aims to 'collapse the distance between academic, critical and creative writing'.

Book series

These book series publish book-length fiction based on research.

- *ethnoGRAPHIC* book series from the University of Toronto Press: publishes graphic novels based on anthropological research (*Lissa* was published by this press, and the series editors include Sherine Hamdy).
- *Social Fictions* series from Brill/Sense: publishes sociologically informed novels (edited by Patricia Leavy).

Other resources

Databases, blogs and resources relating to research and fiction. These may be useful to researchers searching for published fiction that connects to their work.

- Bad Bugs Book Club, based at Manchester Metropolitan University, UK. This online book club facilitates discussions about popular fiction (and non-fiction) concerning microbiology and infectious diseases (see also Verran 2013). https://www.mmu.ac.uk/engage/what-we-do/bad-bugs-bookclub/
- *Lablit: The Culture of Science in Fiction and Fact*. Online repository of fiction about scientists and laboratory work. https://lablit.com
- London Arts-Based Research Centre. This arts-based research organisation 'offers a wide range of inspiring projects, conferences, courses, workshops, as well as creative research opportunities for writers, scholars, academics and artists around the world'. https://labrc.co.uk/about/

- MATHFICT. An online database of fiction about maths and mathematicians. http://kasmana.people.cofc.edu/MATHFICT/
- *The Sociological Review*'s blog publishes reviews of popular fiction from a sociological perspective.

Creating your own forum for dissemination

Some researchers who have used fiction in their own research have taken a step beyond self-publication and set up a new forum for disseminating research-inspired fiction. Several of the more specialised publications listed in Box 6.1 were created by researchers who use fiction in their work. For example, *SoFi Zine* was created by Ash Watson and the *Social Fictions* book series is edited by Patricia Leavy, both key figures and advocates of social-science fiction. These innovations were perhaps inspired by the absence of alternative suitable forums through which to publish their own, and colleagues', work.

While the work involved in advocating for and setting up new publication avenues should not be underestimated, we highlight these examples in order to demonstrate that the history of research-fiction is one of experimentation and innovation. This can involve pushing at disciplinary boundaries and expanding what counts as research and research outputs. If researchers cannot find a suitable forum in which to share their research-fiction, they may wish to consider creating something new.

Concluding thoughts

In this chapter, we have discussed a number of ways in which researchers may choose to share research-fictions with audiences outside of their immediate team of colleagues and/or research participants: performance, self-publication and literary or academic/professional publications. We have highlighted various benefits and limitations (for example, costs, accessibility, reach and visibility) which researchers should consider when deciding which (if any) of these avenues is the right one for them and their research.

In conjunction with Chapter 5, we hope this will give readers some practical ideas about how they can go about creating and sharing research-fictions (if indeed that is their aim). However, we hope that it will now be clear that there is no one 'right' way to do or share research-fiction. Instead, when thinking about publication and dissemination, as with all aspects of the research journey, the key is to consider the overall aims of the research endeavour and the rationale for employing fiction. The specific paths a researcher takes and the tools they put to use should align with the researcher's vision for where this journey should take them (and their stakeholders) – while allowing for some surprises along the way!

Reflective questions

- Who needs to engage with your research in order for you to achieve your objectives?
- What existing publications, platforms and forums exist where you might reach these audiences?
- How will the different publication or performance avenues you are considering impact the accessibility and inclusivity of your research?
- Is there a need for a new forum for research-fiction in your discipline or research area? What might this look like?

Notes

Chapter 1

1. Hurston's writing has been the subject of much scholarship, some of which examines the relation between her academic work and literary outputs. For instance, Patricia Leavy offers an overview of Hurston's work through this lens (2022: 21–22), and see Henry Louis Gates' (2013) afterword in *Their Eyes*. Hurston also reflects on some of these issues in her autobiography, *Dust Tracks on a Road* (1996).
2. Of course these 'what if?' questions – speculations about unlikely or impossible things – can plant the seeds from which 'works of fiction' grow. As a character in one of Lorrie Moore's short stories observes, 'this is the kind of thing that fiction is: it's the unliveable life, the strange room tacked onto the house, the extra moon that is circling the earth unbeknownst to science' (Moore 1999: 235).
3. While much of the discussion in this book concerns prose fiction, graphic novels and performances, we would suggest that many, if not most, of the fictional stories that people ordinarily encounter and consume are on-screen.

Chapter 2

1. Throughout this book, we use the terms 'research-fiction/s' and 'research-based fiction' to refer to any fiction which arises from a research project. See also Chapter 4 for a more detailed discussion of terminology.

Chapter 3

1. Since our focus is on how researchers can employ fiction in the production and communication of research, it is beyond the scope of this book to fully explore the pedagogical potentials of fiction. However, many scholars have explored the use of novels and other fictional works to explain concepts and theories to students of all ages, in the social sciences and beyond (a detailed discussion can be found in Leavy 2013: 259–276; see also Verran 2013; Watson 2016; Yazell et al 2021; Oziewicz 2023).
2. Considerations of fiction are, of course, commonplace in disciplines such as media and cultural studies or literature, where fictional outputs may be analysed in relation to the cultures in which they are embedded. However, our focus here is on disciplinary contexts where 'thinking with fiction' as a form of research is more unusual.

[3] The story discussed here can be viewed on the project website: https://stories2connect.org

Chapter 4

[1] We would add an observation that fictions drawing on social research are frequently published in methodologically focussed outlets (for example, *Qualitative Inquiry* or *Qualitative Research*). Although these are important contributions to the research community, there may be a risk that such work is framed as primarily *methodological* and consequently read and cited by those interested in fiction as *method*, rather than contributing to conversations about substantive findings.

References

Ahern, C. (2019) *Roar*, New York: Grand Central Publishing.
Amos, M. and Page, R. (eds) (2014) *Beta-Life: Stories from an A-Life Future*, Manchester: Comma Press.
Anderson, M. (2007) 'Making Theatre from Data: Lessons for Performance Ethnography from Verbatim Theatre', *NJ: Drama Australia Journal*, 31(1): 79–91.
Appignanesi, J. (director) (2012) *Rufus Stone*, [online] available at: https://vimeo.com/109360805
Aristotle (1997) *Poetics*, Mineola: Dover Publications.
Ball, D. (1983) *Backwards and Forwards: A Technical Manual for Reading Plays*, Carbondale: Southern Illinois University Press.
Banks, A. and Banks, S. (eds) (1998) *Fiction and Social Research: By Ice or Fire*, Walnut Creek: AltaMira Press.
Barone, T. and Eisner, E. (2012) *Arts Based Research*, Thousand Oaks: SAGE.
Bassett, C., Steinmueller, E. and Voss, G. (2013) 'Better Made Up: The Mutual Influence of Science Fiction and Innovation', NESTA Working Paper Series, [online] available at: https://media.nesta.org.uk/documents/better_made_up_the_mutual_influence_of_science_fiction_and_innovation.pdf
Berger, J. (1972) *G.*, New York: Viking Press.
Bettelheim, B. (1989) *The Uses of Enchantment: The Meaning and Importance of Fairy Tales*, New York: Vintage.
Bleecker, J. (2009) *Design Fiction: A Short Essay on Design, Science, Fact, and Fiction*, Near Future Laboratory, [online] available at: https://systemsorienteddesign.net/wp-content/uploads/2011/01/DesignFiction_WebEdition.pdf
Blum, J. (2004) *Those Who Save Us*, Orlando: Harcourt.
Blum, J. (2018) *The Lost Family*, New York: HarperCollins.
Blythe, A. (2014) *Little Revolution (NHB Modern Drama)*, London: Nick Hern Books.

Boal, A. (1995) *The Rainbow of Desire: The Boal Method of Theatre and Therapy*, London: Routledge.

Boal, A. (2002) *Games for Actors and Non-Actors* (2nd edn), New York: Routledge.

Bochner, A. (2000) 'Criteria Against Ourselves', *Qualitative Inquiry*, 6(2): 266–272.

Bohannan, L. (1966) 'Shakespeare in the Bush', *Natural History*, August-September: 28–33.

Bowen, E.S. (1964) *Return to Laughter: An Anthropological Novel*, New York: Anchor Books.

Braun, V., Clarke, V., Hayfield, N., Frith, H., Malson, H.M. and Shah-Beckley, I. (2019) 'Qualitative Story Completion: Possibilities and Potential Pitfalls', *Qualitative Research in Psychology*, 16(1): 136–155.

Breen, J. (2017) 'Disability as Difference: A Fictional Representation', *The Qualitative Report*, 22(10, article 8): 2722–2741.

Bricklebank, P. (2006) 'Personal Essay and Memoir' in New York Writers Workshop (eds) *The Portable MFA in Creative Writing*, Cincinnati: Writer's Digest Books, pp 76–135.

Brockes, E. (2019) 'Cat Person Author Kristen Roupenian: "Dating Is Caught up in Ego, Power and Control"', *The Guardian*, 26 January, [online] available at: https://www.theguardian.com/books/2019/jan/26/cat-person-author-kristen-roupenian-dating-ego-power-control

Brotzel, D. (2019) 'Active and Passive Voice', *Pithead Chapel*, 8(9), [online] available at: https://pitheadchapel.com/active-and-passive-voice/

Bruce, T. (2019) 'The Case for Faction as a Potent Method for Integrating Fact and Fiction in Research' in S. Farquhar and E. Fitzpatrick (eds) *Innovations in Narrative and Metaphor*, Singapore: Springer, pp 57–72.

Bruner, J. (2002) *Acts of Meaning*, Cambridge: Harvard University Press.

Bryanston, C. and Lewando Hundt, G. (nd) 'Performing Research as Ethnodrama: Passing On', *Warwick Open Space Learning*, [online] available at: https://warwick.ac.uk/fac/cross_fac/iatl/resources/outputs-old/osl/ethnodrama/case_study/

Burawoy, M. (2005) 'For Public Sociology', *American Sociological Review*, 70(1): 4–28.

Cahill, H. (2010) 'Re-Thinking the Fiction–Reality Boundary: Investigating the Use of Drama in HIV Prevention Projects in Vietnam', *Research in Drama Education: The Journal of Applied Theatre and Performance*, 15(2): 155–174.

Cambridge English Dictionary (2023) 'Story' and 'Narrative', University of Cambridge Press, [online] available at: https://dictionary.cambridge.org/dictionary/english/story and https://dictionary.cambridge.org/dictionary/english/narrative

Cameron, J. (2016) *The Artist's Way: A Spiritual Path to Higher Creativity*, New York: TarcherPeregree.

Casement, W. (1987) 'Literature and Didacticism: Examining Some Popularly Held Ideas', *The Journal of Aesthetic Education*, 21(1): 101–111.

Castronova, E. (2006) 'On the Research Value of Large Games: Natural Experiments in Norrath and Camelot', *Games and Culture*, 1(2): 163–186.

Christensen, J. (2009) 'The Komatik Lesson', *The Northern Review*, 31(fall): 125–135.

Christensen, J. (2012) 'Telling Stories: Exploring Research Storytelling as a Meaningful Approach to Knowledge Mobilization with Indigenous Research Collaborators and Diverse Audiences in Community-Based Participatory Research', *The Canadian Geographer / Le Géographe Canadien*, 56(2): 231–242.

Clanchy, K. (2015) *The Not-Dead and the Saved and Other Stories*, London: Picador.

Clarke, V. and Braun, V. (2019) 'How Can a Heterosexual Man Remove His Body Hair and Retain His Masculinity? Mapping Stories of Male Body Hair Depilation', *Qualitative Research in Psychology*, 16(1): 96–114.

Clarke, V., Braun, V., Frith, H. and Moller, N. (2019) 'Editorial Introduction to the Special Issue: *Using Story Completion Methods in Qualitative Research*', *Qualitative Research in Psychology*, 16(1): 1–20.

Clifford, J. and Marcus, G.E. (1986) *Writing Culture: The Poetics and Politics of Ethnography*, Berkeley: University of California Press.

Cohn, D. (1999) *The Distinction of Fiction*, Baltimore: Johns Hopkins University Press.

Conrad, D. (2023) 'Engagement, Authenticity, and Advocacy in "Youth Uncensored": Ethics in Applied Theater Research With Street-Involved Youth', *Qualitative Inquiry*, 29(2): 365–373.

Crockett Thomas, P. (2022) *Abolition Sci-Fi*, [downloadable booklet] available at: https://abolitionscifi.org/

Crockett Thomas, P., McNeill, F., Cathcart Frödén, L., Collinson Scott, J., Escobar, O. and Urie, A. (2021) 'Re-Writing Punishment? Songs and Narrative Problem-Solving', *Incarceration* 2(1).

Davies, K. (2023) *Siblings and Sociology*, Manchester: Manchester University Press.

Davis, A. (2022) 'Writing and Birthing on Country: Examining Indigenous Australian Birth Stories from a Reproductive Justice Lens' in B.W. Capo and L. Lazzari (eds) *The Palgrave Handbook of Reproductive Justice and Literature*, Cham: Springer, pp 333–355.

Davis, C., Senechal, M. and Zwicky, J. (eds) (2008) *The Shape of Content: Creative Writing in Mathematics and Science*, Wellesley: AK Peters.

Denzin, N.K. (1997) *Interpretive Ethnography: Ethnographic Practices for the 21st Century*, Thousand Oaks: SAGE.

Derrida, J. and Spivak, G.C. (1976) *Of Grammatology*, Baltimore: Johns Hopkins University Press.

Diversi, M. (1998) 'Glimpses of Street Life: Representing Lived Experience Through Short Stories', *Qualitative Inquiry*, 4(2): 131–147.

Douedari, Y., Alhaffar, M., Duclos, D., Al-Twaish, M., Jabbour, S. and Howard, N. (2021) '"We Need Someone to Deliver Our Voices": Reflections from Conducting Remote Qualitative Research in Syria', *Conflict and Health*, 15(28): 1–10.

Douglas, K. and Carless, D. (2009) 'Exploring Taboo Issues in Professional Sport through a Fictional Approach', *Reflective Practice*, 10(3): 311–323.

Dumitrica, D.D. (2010) 'Choosing Methods, Negotiating Legitimacy: A Metalogue on Autoethnography', *Graduate Journal of Social Science*, 7(1).

Elphinstone, M. and Wickham-Jones, C. (2012) 'Archaeology and Fiction', *Antiquity*, 86(332): 532–537.

Ensler, E. (1998) *The Vagina Monologues*, New York: Villard Books.

Ernaux, A. (2017) *The Years* (trans A. Strayer), New York: Seven Stories Press.

Facca, D., Gladstone, B. and Teachman, G. (2020) 'Working the Limits of "Giving Voice" to Children: A Critical Conceptual Review', *International Journal of Qualitative Methods*, 19.

Falk, D. (2017) 'Armchair Science: Thought Experiments Played a Crucial Role in the History of Science. But Do They Tell Us Anything about the Real World?' *Aeon*, 20 December, [online] available at: https://aeon.co/essays/do-thought-experiments-really-uncover-new-scientific-truths

Fall, J. (2021) 'Worlds of Vision: Thinking Geographically through Comics', *ACME: An International Journal for Critical Geographies*, 20(1): 17–33.

Farrant, F. (2014) 'Unconcealment: What Happens When We Tell Stories', *Qualitative Inquiry*, 20(4): 461–470.

Fenge, L., Jones, K. and Gibson, C. (2018) 'Meaningful Dissemination Produces the "Long Tail" That Engenders Community Impact', *Qualitative Research Journal*, 18(1): 45–54.

Flood, A. (2018) 'US Losing Appetite for Reading Fiction, Research Finds', *The Guardian*, 17 September, [online] available at: https://www.theguardian.com/books/2018/sep/17/us-losing-appetite-for-reading-fiction-research-finds

Foucault, M. (1998) *The History of Sexuality. Vol. 1, The Will to Knowledge*, London: Penguin.

Fox, K. (2021) 'A Funny Turn' in R. Phillips and H. Kara, *Creative Writing for Social Research*, Bristol: Policy Press, pp 159–163.

Fox, M. (2020) 'From Folktale to Fantasy: A Recipe-Based Approach to Creative Writing', *Writing in Practice: The Journal of Creative Writing Research*, 6.

Frank, K. (2000) '"The Management of Hunger": Using Fiction in Writing Anthropology', *Qualitative Inquiry*, 6(4): 474–488.

Gaffney, D. (2013) 'Get Shorty' in V. Gebbie (ed) *Short Circuit*, Cromer: Salt, pp 162–168.

Gaiman, N. (2016) *The View from the Cheap Seats: A Collection of Introductions, Essays, and Assorted Writings*, New York: William Morrow.

Gallese, V. and Wojciehowski, H. (2011) 'How Stories Make Us Feel: Toward an Embodied Narratology', *California Italian Studies*, 2(1).

Gardner, J. (1991) *The Art of Fiction: Notes on Craft for Young Writers*, New York: Vintage.

Gates, H.L. (2013 [1937]) 'Afterword' in Z.N. Hurston, *Their Eyes Were Watching God*, New York: HarperPerennial Modern Classics, pp 195–205.

Gebbie, V. (ed) (2013) *Short Circuit: A Guide to the Art of the Short Story*, Cromer: Salt.

Geertz, C. (2017) *The Interpretation of Cultures: Selected Essays* (3rd edn), New York: Basic Books.

Gembus, M.P. (2018) 'The Safe Spaces "In-between": Plays, Performance and Identity among Young "Second Generation" Somalis in London', *Children's Geographies*, 16(4): 432–443.

Gergen, K. and Gergen, M. (1988) 'Narratives and the Self as Relationship', *Advances in Experimental Social Psychology*, 21: 17–56.

Gibson, W. (2021) 'Aesthetics, Verisimilitude and User Engagement: Reporting Findings through Fictional Accounts in Qualitative Inquiry', *Qualitative Research*, 21(5): 650–666.

Goldberg, N. (1986) *Writing Down the Bones: Freeing the Writer Within*, Boston: Shambhala.

Goldberg, N. (1991) *Wild Mind: Living the Writer's Life*, London: Rider.

Hamdy, S. and Nye, C. (illustrated by Bao, S. and Brewer, C., lettering by Parenteau, M.) (2017) *Lissa: A Story about Medical Promise, Friendship, and Revolution*, North York: University of Toronto Press.

Hammond, W. and Steward, D. (2012) *Verbatim, Verbatim: Contemporary Documentary Theatre*, London: Bloomsbury Publishing.

Haraway, D. (1988) 'Situated Knowledges: The Science Question in Feminism and the Privilege of Partial Perspective', *Feminist Studies*, 14(3): 575–599.

Haraway, D. (1991) *Simians, Cyborgs and Women: The Reinvention of Nature*, New York: Routledge.

Haraway, D. (2016) *Staying with the Trouble: Making Kin in the Chthulucene*, Durham: Duke University Press.

Harding, S. (1993) 'Rethinking Standpoint Epistemology: What Is "Strong Objectivity"' in L. Alcoff and E. Potter (eds) *Feminist Epistemologies*, London: Routledge, pp 49–82.

Haurant, S. (2022) 'How to Get Your Own Book Published: A Step by Step Guide', *The Guardian*, 9 August, [online] available at: https://www.theguardian.com/money/2022/aug/09/how-to-get-your-own-book-published-a-step-by-step-guide

Hecht, T. (2017) 'Denial: A Visit in Four Ethnographic Fictions' in A. Pandian and S. McLean (eds) *Crumpled Paper Boat*, Durham: Duke University Press, pp 130–144.

Helden, D.v. and Witcher, R. (eds) (2020) *Researching the Archaeological Past through Imagined Narratives: A Necessary Fiction*, Abingdon: Routledge.

Hershman, T. (2013) 'Art Breathes from Containment' in V. Gebbie (ed) *Short Circuit*, Cromer: Salt, pp 169–178.

Hill Collins, P. (2014) *Black Feminist Thought: Knowledge, Consciousness, and the Politics of Empowerment* (10th anniversary edn), Abingdon: Routledge.

Hirshfield, J. (2012) 'The Art of the Metaphor', *TED*, [online animation] available at: https://ed.ted.com/lessons/jane-hirshfield-the-art-of-the-metaphor

Holstein, J.A. and Gubrium, J.F. (2000) *The Self We Live by: Narrative Identity in a Postmodern World*, Oxford: Oxford University Press.

Humphrey, H. (photographer) (2023) *AS IS film: A Play Based on Research about Trans, Intersex and LGBTI Activist Relationships*, Children and Young People's Centre for Justice, University of Strathclyde, [online] (link available on request from author).

Humphrey, H., Taylor, Y. and Govender, N. (2023) *AS IS; Access and Inclusion in KE Events*, Children and Young People's Centre for Justice, University of Strathclyde, [online report] available at: https://pureportal.strath.ac.uk/files/157364011/Humphrey_etal_2023_AS_IS_Access_inclusion_KE_events.pdf

Hurston, Z.N. (1996) *Dust Tracks on a Road*, New York: HarperPerennial.

Hurston, Z.N. (2013 [1937]) *Their Eyes Were Watching God*, New York: HarperPerennial Modern Classics.

Imarisha, W., brown, a.m. and Thomas, S.R. (2015) *Octavia's Brood*, Oakland: AK Press.

Inckle, K. (2007) *Writing on the Body? Thinking through Gendered Embodiment and Marked Flesh*, Newcastle upon Tyne: Cambridge Scholars.

Inckle, K. (2010) 'Telling Tales? Using Ethnographic Fictions to Speak Embodied "Truth"', *Qualitative Research*, 10(1): 27–47.

Jones, K. (2013) 'Infusing Biography with the Personal: Writing Rufus Stone', *Creative Approaches to Research*, 6(2): 2–23.

Kang, A.R., Blackburn, J., Kwak, H. and Kim, H.K (2017) 'I Would Not Plant Apple Trees If the World Will Be Wiped: Analyzing Hundreds of Millions of Behavioral Records of Players During an MMORPG Beta Test' in *Proceedings of the 26th International World Wide Web Conference*, Geneva: International World Wide Web Conferences Steering Committee, pp 435–444.

Kara, H. (2013) 'It's Hard to Tell How Research Feels: Using Fiction to Enhance Academic Research and Writing', *Qualitative Research in Organizations and Management: An International Journal*, 8(1): 70–84.

Karasik, P. (2017) 'Afterword: reading *Lissa*' in S. Hamdy and C. Nye, *Lissa*, North York: University of Toronto Press, pp 241–50.

Keen, S. (2006) 'A Theory of Narrative Empathy', *NARRATIVE*, 14(3): 207–237.

King, S. (2010) *On Writing: A Memoir of the Craft*, New York: Scribner.

Kuhn, T.S. (1970) *The Structure of Scientific Revolutions* (2nd edn), Chicago: Chicago University Press.

Lackey, M. (2016) 'Locating and Defining the Bio in Biofiction', *A/b: Auto/Biography Studies*, 31(1): 3–10.

Lafrenière, D. and Cox, S.M. (2013) '"If You Can Call It a Poem": Toward a Framework for the Assessment of Arts-Based Works', *Qualitative Research*, 13(3): 318–336.

Lamott, A. (2019) *Bird by Bird: Some Instructions on Writing and Life*, New York: Anchor Books.

Leavy, P. (2012) 'Fiction and Critical Perspectives on Social Research: A Research Note', *Humanity & Society*, 36(3): 251–259.

Leavy, P. (2013) *Fiction as Research Practice: Short Stories, Novellas, and Novels*, Walnut Creek: Left Coast Press.

Leavy, P. (2019) *Spark*, New York: The Guilford Press.

Leavy, P. (2022) *Re/Invention: Methods of Social Fiction*, New York: The Guilford Press.

References

Le Guin, U.K. (2015) *Steering the Craft: A Twenty-First Century Guide to Sailing the Sea of Story*, New York: Mariner Books.

Lenette, C., Brough, M., Schweitzer, R.D., Correa-Velez, I., Murray, K. and Vromans, L. (2019) '"Better than a Pill": Digital Storytelling as a Narrative Process for Refugee Women', *Media Practice and Education*, 20(1): 67–86.

Lepenies, W. (1988) *Between Literature and Science: The Rise of Sociology*, Cambridge: Cambridge University Press.

Lewando Hundt, G., Stuttaford, M.C., Bryanston, C. and Harrison, C. (2019) '"Research Usually Sits on Shelves, Through the Play It Was Shared": Co-Producing Knowledge Through Post-Show Discussions of Research-Based Theatre', *Frontiers in Sociology*, 4(48).

Lewis, P.A. and Page, R. (eds) (2015) *Spindles: Stories from the New Science of Sleep*, Manchester: Comma Press.

Lightman, A. (1993) *Einstein's Dreams*, New York: Pantheon Books.

Lord, C., Ellsworth-Krebs, K. and Holmes, T. (2023) '"Telling Tales": Communicating UK Energy Research through Fairy Tale Characters', *Energy Research & Social Science*, 101: 103100.

Lyotard, J.-F. (1984) *The Postmodern Condition: A Report on Knowledge*, Minneapolis: University of Minnesota Press.

Macleod, A. (2013) 'Writing and Risk Taking' in V. Gebbie (ed) *Short Circuit*, Cromer: Salt, pp 4–13.

Marek, A. (2013) 'What My Gland Wants: Originality in the Short Story' in V. Gebbie (ed) *Short Circuit*, Cromer: Salt, pp 145–151.

Markham, A. (2012) 'Fabrication as Ethical Practice: Qualitative Inquiry in Ambiguous Internet Contexts', *Information, Communication & Society*, 15(3): 334–353.

Martin, E. (1991) 'The Egg and the Sperm: How Science Has Constructed a Romance Based on Stereotypical Male-Female Roles', *Signs*, 16(3): 485–501.

Mason, J. (2002) *Qualitative Researching* (2nd edn), Thousand Oaks: SAGE.

Mason, J. (2018) *Affinities: Potent Connections in Personal Life*, Cambridge: Polity.

May, V. (2008) 'On Being a "Good" Mother: The Moral Presentation of Self in Written Life Stories', *Sociology*, 42(3): 470–486.

Mazzei, L.A. and Jackson, A.Y. (2012) 'Complicating Voice in a Refusal to "Let Participants Speak for Themselves"', *Qualitative Inquiry*, 18(9): 745–751.

McCloud, S. (1994) *Understanding Comics*, New York: HarperPerennial.

McKee, R. (1997) *Story: Substance, Structure, Style and the Principles of Screenwriting*, New York: ReganBooks.

McMillan, A. and McNicol, S. (2021) 'Working with What's There' in R. Phillips and H. Kara, *Creative Writing for Social Research*, Bristol: Policy Press, pp 86–89.

McNicol, S. (2019) 'Using Participant-Created Comics as a Research Method', *Qualitative Research Journal*, 19(3): 236–247.

McSweeney, T. and Joy, S. (eds) (2019) *Through the Black Mirror: Deconstructing the Side Effects of the Digital Age*, Cham: Palgrave Macmillan.

Moore, L. (1999) *Birds of America: Stories*, New York: Picador.

Murdoch, I. (1999) *Existentialists and Mystics: Writings on Philosophy and Literature*, London: Penguin.

Nadar, S. (2014) '"Stories Are Data with Soul": Lessons from Black Feminist Epistemology', *Agenda*, 28(1): 18–28.

Nägele, L.V., Ryöppy, M. and Wilde, D. (2018) 'PDFi: Participatory Design Fiction with Vulnerable Users', *Proceedings of the 10th Nordic Conference on Human-Computer Interaction*, New York: Association for Computing Machinery, pp 819–831.

Nesta (2015) *Infectious Futures: Stories of the Post-Antibiotic Apocalypse*, [downloadable booklet] available at: https://www.nesta.org.uk/report/longitude-prize-infectious-futures/

Netolicky, D.M. (2019) 'Redefining Leadership in Schools: The Cheshire Cat as Unconventional Metaphor', *Journal of Educational Administration and History*, 51(2): 149–164.

Newberger Goldstein, R. and Lightman, A. (2011) 'Bridging the Two Cultures: A Conversation between Alan Lightman and Rebecca Newberger Goldstein', *World Literature Today*, 85(1): 30–35.

North, K. (2017) 'Exploring Care for Children with Autism in Wales Using Creative Writing as a Research Method in a Collaborative Pilot Study', *Writing in Practice: The Journal of Creative Writing Research*, 3.

Nussbaum, M.C. (2007) *Poetic Justice: The Literary Imagination and Public Life*, Boston: Beacon Press.

Oakley, A. (1988) *The Men's Room*, London: Virago.

Osei-Tutu, A.A.Z. (2023) 'Developing African Oral Traditional Storytelling as a Framework for Studying with African Peoples', *Qualitative Research*, 23(6): 1497–1514

Oziewicz, M. (2023) 'CLICK Framework: A Care-Centric Conceptual Map for Organizing Climate Literacy Pedagogy', *Climate Literacy in Education*, 1(2): 44–50.

Page, R. (ed) (2012) *Bio-Punk: Stories from the Far Side of Research*, Manchester: Comma Press.

Pandian, A. and McLean, S. (eds) (2017) *Crumpled Paper Boat: Experiments in Ethnographic Writing*, Durham: Duke University Press.

Park-Kang, S. (2015) 'Fictional IR and Imagination: Advancing Narrative Approaches', *Review of International Studies*, 41(2): 361–381.

Parr, H. (2021) 'Where Sophie's Story Went Next: The Banal Afterlife of an Applied Cultural Geography' in R. Phillips and H. Kara *Creative Writing for Social Research*, Bristol: Policy Press, pp 167–171.

Penfold-Mounce, R., Beer, D. and Burrows, R. (2011) '*The Wire* as Social Science-Fiction?' *Sociology*, 45(1): 152–167.

Phillips, R. and Kara, H. (2021) *Creative Writing for Social Research: A Practical Guide*, Bristol: Policy Press.

Phillips, R., Ali, N. and Chambers, C. (2020) 'Critical Collaborative Storying: Making an Animated Film about Halal Dating', *Cultural Geographies*, 27(1): 37–54.

Plummer, K. (2001) *Documents of Life 2: An Invitation to a Critical Humanism*, Thousand Oaks: SAGE.

Policarpo, V. (2018) 'Taking the Risk? Literary Writing and Sociology', paper presented at *Everyday Creativity: A Morgan Centre Conference*, University of Manchester, 10–11 July.

Polkinghorne, D.E. (1988) *Narrative Knowing and the Human Sciences*, Albany: SUNY Press.

Ponzio, P. (2021) 'Dickens and Society: Can Dickens's "Uppers" Change Their Minds?' in G. McMillan (ed) *The Routledge Companion to Literature and Class*, New York: Routledge, pp 91–104.

Popova, M. (2019) 'How Kepler Invented Science Fiction and Defended His Mother in a Witchcraft Trial While Revolutionizing Our Understanding of the Universe', *The Marginalian*, 26 December, [online] available at: https://www.themarginalian.org/2019/12/26/katharina-kepler-witchcraft-dream/

Rabbiosi, C. and Vanolo, A. (2017) 'Are We Allowed to Use Fictional Vignettes in Cultural Geographies?', *Cultural Geographies*, 24(2): 265–278.

Rautio, P. (2022) 'Four Stories of Significant Animal Relations – Four Friendships?', paper presented at *CLAN Conference: Children-Animal Friendships*, University of Lisbon, 22 September.

Raynor, R. (2016) *Holding Things Together (And What Falls Apart ...): Encountering and Dramatizing Austerity with Women in the North East of England*, PhD thesis, Durham University.

Raynor, R. (2019) 'Speaking, Feeling, Mattering: Theatre as Method and Model for Practice-Based, Collaborative, Research', *Progress in Human Geography*, 43(4): 691–710.

Repp, C. (2012) 'What's Wrong with Didacticism?', *The British Journal of Aesthetics*, 52(3): 271–285.

Rhodes, C. and Brown, A.D. (2005) 'Writing Responsibly: Narrative Fiction and Organization Studies', *Organization*, 12(4): 467–491.

Richardson, L. (1993) 'Poetics, Dramatics, and Transgressive Validity: The Case of the Skipped Line', *The Sociological Quarterly*, 34(4): 695–710.

Richardson, L. (1997a) *Fields of Play: Constructing an Academic Life*, New Brunswick: Rutgers University Press.

Richardson, L. (1997b) 'Skirting a Pleated Text: De-Disciplining an Academic Life', *Qualitative Inquiry*, 3(3): 295–303.

Richardson, L. and St. Pierre, E. (2005) 'Writing: A Method of Inquiry' in N. Denzin and Y. Lincoln (eds) *The SAGE Handbook of Qualitative Research* (3rd edn), Thousand Oaks: SAGE, pp 959–978.

Riessman, C.K. (1993) *Narrative Analysis*, London: SAGE.

Roupenian, K. (2017) 'Cat Person', *The New Yorker*, 4 December, [online] available at: https://www.newyorker.com/magazine/2017/12/11/cat-person

Ruhl, S. (2008) *Eurydice*, New York: Samuel French.

Ryman, G. (2010) *When It Changed: Science into Fiction: An Anthology*, Manchester: Comma Press.

Sagan, C. (1985) *Contact*, New York: Simon and Schuster.

Said, E.W. (1994) *Orientalism*, New York: Vintage.

Saldaña, J. (ed) (2005) *Ethnodrama: An Anthology of Reality Theatre*, Walnut Creek: AltaMira Press.

References

Salesses, M. (2021) *Craft in the Real World: Rethinking Fiction Writing and Workshopping*, New York: Catapult.

Satchwell, C., Watson, D., Blatch, K., Brown, M., Davidge, G., Evans, N., Howard, M., Larkins, C., Piccini, H., Thomas-Hughes, H. and Violet, A. (2018) *Collaborative Fiction Writing with Community Groups: A Practitioner Guide*, [downloadable booklet] available at: https://connected-communities.org/index.php/project_resources/collaborative-fiction-writing-with-community-groups-a-practitioner-guide/

Satchwell, C., Larkins, C., Davidge, D. and Carter, B. (2020) 'Stories as Findings in Collaborative Research: Making Meaning through Fictional Writing with Disadvantaged Young People', *Qualitative Research*, 20(6): 874–891.

Schmidt, N. (1984) 'Ethnographic Fiction: Anthropology's Hidden Literary Style', *Anthropology and Humanism Quarterly*, 9(4): 11–14.

Self, W. (2014) 'A Point of View: Why Orwell Was a Literary Mediocrity', *bbc.com*, 31 August, [online] available at: https://www.bbc.com/news/magazine-28971276

Shah, S. and Greer, S. (2018) 'Polio Monologues: Translating Ethnographic Text into Verbatim Theatre', *Qualitative Research*, 18(1): 53–69.

Simms, A. (2017) *Knock Twice: 25 Modern Folktales for Troubling Times*, Real Press/New Weather Institute.

Smith, K.E., Bandola-Gill, J., Meer, N., Stewart, E. and Watermeyer, R. (2020) *The Impact Agenda: Controversies, Consequences and Challenges*, Bristol: Policy Press.

Snow, C.P. (2012) *The Two Cultures*, Cambridge: Cambridge University Press.

Sou, G. and Cei Douglas, J. (2019) *After Maria: Everyday Recovery After Disaster*, University of Manchester, [downloadable comic] available at: https://www.hcri.manchester.ac.uk/research/projects/after-maria/

Sousanis, N. (2015) *Unflattening*, Cambridge: Harvard University Press.

South, M. (2020) 'Frequently Asked Questions about Your Craniotomy', *The White Review*, January, [online] available at: https://www.thewhitereview.org/fiction/frequently-asked-questions-craniotomy/

STAMP: Theatre and Media Productions CIC (nd) '"Passing On" Santé Theatre Warwick in association with Little Angel Theatre presents Passing On by Mike Kenny', [project website] available at: https://www.stamproductions.co.uk/past-productions/passing-on

Storr, W. (2020) *The Science of Storytelling: Why Stories Make Us Human and How to Tell Them Better*, New York: Abrams Books.

Stuart, M.T., Fehige, Y. and Brown, J.R. (2018) *The Routledge Companion to Thought Experiments*, Abingdon: Routledge.

Sudarsan, I., Hoare, K., Sheridan, N. and Roberts, J. (2022) 'Giving Voice to Children in Research: The Power of Child-centered Constructivist Grounded Theory Methodology', *Research in Nursing & Health*, 45(4): 488–497.

Taylor, J., Namey, E., Carrington Johnson, A. and Guest, G. (2017) 'Beyond the Page: A Process Review of Using Ethnodrama to Disseminate Research Findings', *Journal of Health Communication*, 22(6): 532–544.

Tipper, B. and Gilman, L. (2019) *Going Home: Short Stories about Egg Sharing, Inspired by Research*, University of Manchester, [downloadable booklet] available at: https://pure.manchester.ac.uk/ws/portalfiles/portal/157801566/Going_Home_Short_Stories_about_Egg_Sharing_Inspired_by_Research.pdf

Tipper, B. and Gilman, L. (2020) 'Three Stories About Egg Sharing', *The Sociological Review Magazine*, 25 June, [online] available at: https://thesociologicalreview.org/fiction/three-stories-about-egg-sharing

Tipper, B. and Gilman, L. (2022) *Known Unknowns: Short Stories about Known Egg Donation, Inspired by Research*, University of Manchester, [downloadable booklet] available at: https://pure.manchester.ac.uk/ws/portalfiles/portal/227753669/KnownUnknowns.pdf

Toliver, S.R. (2021) *Recovering Black Storytelling in Qualitative Research: Endarkened Storywork*, London: Routledge.

Tomlinson, T. (2006) 'Fiction' in New York Writers Workshop (ed) *The Portable MFA in Creative Writing*, Cincinnati: Writer's Digest Books, pp 11–75.

Vanolo, A. (2016) 'Exploring the Afterlife: Relational Spaces, Absent Presences, and Three Fictional Vignettes', *Space and Culture*, 19(2): 192–201.

References

Verran, J. (2013) 'The Bad Bugs Book Club: Science, Literacy, and Engagement', *Journal of Microbiology & Biology Education*, 14(1): 110–112.

Vickers, M.H. (2010) 'The Creation of Fiction to Share Other Truths and Different Viewpoints: A Creative Journey and an Interpretive Process', *Qualitative Inquiry*, 16(7): 556–565.

Vogel, P. (2018) *How I Learned to Drive*, New York: Theatre Communications Group.

Vogler, C. (2007) *The Writer's Journey: Mythic Structure for Writers*, Studio City: Michael Wiese Productions.

Warner, S.O. (2021) *Writing the Novella*, Albuquerque: University of New Mexico Press.

Watson, A. (2016) 'Directions for Public Sociology: Novel Writing as a Creative Approach', *Cultural Sociology*, 10(4): 431–447.

Watson, A. (2020) *Into the Sea*, Leiden: Brill.

Watson, A. (2022) 'Writing Sociological Fiction', *Qualitative Research*, 22(3): 337–352.

Watson, C. (2011) 'Staking a Small Claim for Fictional Narratives in Social and Educational Research', *Qualitative Research*, 11(4): 395–408.

Wegener, C. (2014) 'Writing With Phineas: How a Fictional Character From A. S. Byatt Helped Me Turn My Ethnographic Data Into Research Texts', *Cultural Studies ↔ Critical Methodologies*, 14(4): 351–360.

Wells, H.G. (1906) 'The So-Called Science of Sociology', *The Sociological Review*, 3(1): 357–369.

White, H.V. (2000) *Metahistory: The Historical Imagination in Nineteenth-Century Europe*, Baltimore: Johns Hopkins University Press.

Wolf, M. (1992) *A Thrice-Told Tale: Feminism, Postmodernism, and Ethnographic Responsibility*, Stanford: Stanford University Press.

Yaszek, L. (2006) 'Afrofuturism, Science Fiction, and the History of the Future', *Socialism and Democracy*, 20(3): 41–60.

Yazell, B., Petersen, K., Marx, P. and Fessenbecker, P. (2021) 'The Role of Literary Fiction in Facilitating Social Science Research', *Humanities and Social Sciences Communications*, 8(261): 1–8.

Index

A

academic publishing 89, 126, 129–132
academic writing 6–9, 20, 24, 78, 111–112
access see inclusion
African storytelling 26, 37–38, 47–48, 72, 83
Afrofuturism 37–38, 72–73
Ahern, C. 110–111
animation 51, 53
anonymisation 12, 14, 33–34, 91, 101
archaeology 34, 71
arts based research 27, 80–81, 131
Asian fictional traditions 16
audience 94, 126–127
authorship 94

B

biofiction 8, 19
Black feminism 27–28, 30–31, 72
Boal, A. 25, 28, 35–36, 123
bodies see embodiment
Bohannan, L. 47–48
Bowen, E. see Bohannan, L.
Bryanston, C. (with Lewando Hundt, G.) 56–57, 80, 86, 94, 126

C

Cahill, H. 36, 54, 107
catharsis 35–36, 57
change, in fiction 16, 25, 49, 74, 112–115
  see also social change
characters
  composite 12, 33, 58
  creating/writing 8–9, 16–17, 28–30, 65, 74–75, 85, 108–109, 112–114
  in existing works of fiction 46–47

children and young people
  predilection for storytelling 25
  in research-fictions 47, 50, 51–53, 55, 121, 122
  voice/representation in research 24, 91–92
chorus, in theatre 118
Christensen, J. 28, 65, 80, 86
citation practice 79–80
Clanchy, K. 117
Clarke, V. (with Braun, V.) 48–50, 102
Clifford, J. (with Marcus, G.) 31, 33, 66
co-creation see collaboration
collaboration
  researchers and participants 48–55, 50–53, 85, 101–104
  researchers and writers 51–52, 56–57, 70–71, 100–101, 103–104
comedy 36, 107
comics 25, 59–65, 113–114
Comma Press 70, 89, 129
commissioned writers 55–57, 69–70, 101–102
computer games 54
confidentiality see anonymisation
conflict, in fiction 112–113
Conrad, D. 55, 93
consent 92–94
copyright 94
creative non-fiction 19, 68, 86
  publishing 128, 131
creativity 103–104
crisis, in fiction 17
Crockett Thomas, P. 37, 50–51, 103, 106–108
cultural variation, in fiction 15–18, 26–27

D

data analysis, and fiction 47, 78–79
data generation, and fiction 47–51, 57, 78–79

Davies, K. 47
'Denial' (short stories) *see* Hecht, T.
Design Fiction 38, 53
dialogue 118–120
didacticism 83–84, 101
digital platforms 54, 127–128
dilemma, in fiction 17, 114
dissemination 55–72, 88–91, 125–133
Diversi, M. 122
Douglas, K. (with Carless, D.) 127
drabble *see* flash fiction
drama
 research examples 35–36, 54–59, 123, 126–127
 resources 58, 123
 structure 15
dramatic structure *see* story structure
dystopian fiction 38, 70, 71–72, 85, 106

E

Elphinstone, M. (with Wickham-Jones, C.) 71
embodiment/bodies, and fiction 25–26, 28
 see also sensory detail
emotion/empathy 8–10, 24, 28–30, 32, 35, 72, 92
Endarkened Storywork (novel) *see* Toliver, S.R.
engagement 24, 90
Enlightenment, European 11, 28, 72
epigraph *see* paratext
epistemology 11, 26–27, 30–33, 39–40, 67–68
 see also truth claims
Ernaux, A. 117
ethical questions 91–94, 101
ethnodrama 58, 59, 117–118, 119
evaluation/quality, of research-fiction 80–83
evolutionary origins of storytelling 25–26, 69
exegesis *see* paratexts

F

'faction' 68, 86
fairy tales 10, 83, 115
fantasy 106–108
feedback, audience 80, 90–91
feminism/feminist theory 27–28, 30–31, 37, 72

fiction
 definition 13–14
 elements of 15–18
 versus fact 18–21, 27–28, 35, 92
 to 'think with' 14, 35, 45–48
film 58, 127
first person *see* point of view
flash fiction 66, 120–122
 see also short stories
Forum Theatre 36, 54, 56, 58, 107, 123
Frank, K. 68
future 36–38, 50, 54, 69–70, 71–73

G

Gardner, J. 66, 108–109, 112–113
Gibson, W. 83, 89, 92, 126
Gilman, L. (with Tipper, B.) 37, 111, 117, 122
Goldberg, N. 104–105
graphic novels *see* comics

H

Hamdy, S. (with Nye, C.) 59–64, 91, 113–114
Haraway, D. 37, 78
Harding, S. 30–31
health and illness 56–57, 59–64, 66–67, 69–70
Hecht, T. 66–68, 122
Helden, D.v. (with Witcher, R.) 34
hermit crab stories 115–116
hero's journey 15–16, 20, 50, 72, 116
Hill Collins, P. 26–27, 31
Hirshfield, J. 110
humour *see* comedy
Humphrey, H. 58, 126
Hurston, Z.N. 5–6, 135

I

illustration 51–54, 64, 87
 see also comics
imagination 34–38, 66, 106–108
impact 10–11, 80–81
impact agenda 24, 39
improv/improvisational drama 102, 105, 107
Inckle, K. 28, 32, 68, 92
inclusion 24, 90, 102, 103, 126
Infectious Futures (short story collection) *see* Nesta
influence, of fiction on research 12–13, 70–71

Index

Indigenous storytelling 26, 65, 72
inhibitions, overcoming 104–105

J
Jones, K. 58

K
Kang, A. et al 54
Kara, H. 46–47
  see also Phillips, R. (with Kara, H.)
knowledge-making see epistemology

L
Le Guin, U. 16, 17, 18
Leavy, P. 19, 27, 28–29, 59, 79, 80, 81, 85–87, 92, 93, 100, 128, 131, 132
Lenette, C. 54
Lewando Hundt, G. (with Bryanston, C.) 56–57, 80, 86, 94, 126
Lightman, A. 8–10, 19, 109
'literary imagination' 29, 46
literary magazines and publishers 128–129, 130–131
'lyrical sociology' 46

M
marginalised groups/participants 24, 35–36, 51–53, 79, 91–93
Mason, J. 45, 77
McKee, R. 17, 58, 84
McNicol, S. 64
metaphors 110–112
mirror neurons 25–26
Murdoch, I. 6–7, 9–10, 17, 83–84

N
Nägele, L. et al 53
narrative/s 15, 25–26
Native American see Indigenous
Nesta (*Infectious Futures* short story collection) 69–70, 84–85
Netolicky, D. 46
neuroscience 25–26
non-human, imagined in fiction 35, 37, 50, 108
North, K. 48, 121
novels/novellas
  and research 12, 29–30, 45–46, 65, 71–72, 90
  writing and publishing 66, 100, 128
Nussbaum, M. 29, 46

Nye, C. (with Hamdy, S.) 59–64, 91, 113–114

O
online fiction see digital platforms
open-endedness 32–33, 68, 94, 122
outputs see dissemination

P
paratexts 45, 87–89
Park-Kang, S. 34
parody see comedy
participant-created fictions 35–38, 44, 48–55, 71–73, 84–85, 94, 101–104
participatory research 24, 35, 50–55
Passing On (play) see Lewando Hundt. G. and Bryanston, C.
Penfold-Mounce, R. et al 45–46
performances 54, 55–58, 88–89, 126–127
peripeteia 16, 67, 113
Phillips, R. (with Kara, H.) 17, 82
plays see drama
plotting 15–16, 115–116
point of view 116–118
polyvocality 33, 39–40, 94, 122–124
post-colonialism/decolonisation 30–31, 91
post-modernism 30–31, 90
post-structuralism 30–31
process versus product, fiction as 50–51, 82, 100, 125
professional writers see commissioned writers
'public sociology' 24, 90
publishing research-fictions 88–89, 127–131
puppetry 56–57
'psychic distance' 108–109

Q
qualitative research 27–28, 78–79, 81
quality see evaluation

R
race and racism 26–27, 31, 35, 37–38, 65, 71–73
Rautio, P. 50
Raynor, R. 54–55, 85
reflexivity 68, 81, 100
researcher-authored fiction 59–68, 71–73, 100

representation 30–38, 53, 91–93
Richardson, L. 30, 78
 (with St. Pierre, E.) 19, 32–33, 47, 111–112
role-play *see* drama

S

Saldaña, J. 55, 58, 119
Satchwell, C. et al 51–53, 104
satire *see* comedy
science fiction 12, 37, 38, 50–51, 53, 69–70, 71–72, 106–108
scientific research, and fiction 4, 8–9, 12–13, 38, 68–70, 131
second person *see* point of view
self-publishing 127–128
sensitive issues 58, 64, 93, 103
sensory detail, in fiction 108–110
short stories
 research-fiction examples 50–53, 65, 66–70, 72
 writing and publishing 127–129, 130–131
 see also flash fiction
social change/social justice 28–29, 36–38, 71–73, 85, 92
social sciences 11, 27
'sociological imagination' 29, 65
Sou, G. (with Cei Douglas, J.) 64
Sousanis, N. 25, 64
speculation *see* future
speculative fiction 37–38, 50–51, 69–70, 71–72, 106–108
 see also fantasy, science fiction
St. Pierre, E. (with Richardson, L.) 19, 32–33, 47, 111–112
Stories2Connect (project) *see* Satchwell, C. et al
Storr, W. 16, 17, 25, 84, 113, 119
story/stories
 appeal of 25–27
 definition 15
 structure 15–17, 112–115
story completion 48–50, 74, 85
style, fictional 17

T

taboos 107–108
terminology 86–87
theatre/theatrical *see* drama
third person *see* point of view
thought experiments 13–14
Tipper, B. (with Gilman, L.) 37, 111, 117, 122
Toliver, S.R. 71–73, 87, 129
transcripts 119–120
 see also verbatim fiction
truth claims 11, 26–27, 30–33, 39–40, 67–68, 72
 see also epistemology

U

utopian fiction 37–38, 107–108

V

verbatim fictions 56–59, 94, 119–120, 123
voice *see* representation
vulnerable participants *see* marginalized participants

W

warm-up exercises 104–105
Watson, A. 29, 32, 65, 79, 87–88, 90, 100, 109, 132
Watson, C. 36, 45, 87
websites, for sharing research-fiction *see* digital platforms
Wegener, C. 46–47
Wells, H.G. 37, 107
White, H. 31
Wolf, M. 90, 123
workshops, creative writing 102–103
writers-in-residence 101
writing
 craft of 18, 66
 prompts 99–124
 starting to write 103–105
 see also warm up exercises

www.ingramcontent.com/pod-product-compliance
Lightning Source LLC
Chambersburg PA
CBHW071711020426
42333CB00017B/2217